NINE FOR NINE

NINE FOR NINE

THE PENNSYLVANIA MINE RESCUE MIRACLE

ANDREW MORTON

MICHAEL O'MARA BOOKS LIMITED

First published in Great Britain in 2002 by
Michael O'Mara Books Limited
9 Lion Yard, Tremadoc Road
London sw4 7nq

A CIP catalogue record for this book is available from the
British Library

ISBN 1-84317-013-2

1 3 5 7 9 10 8 6 4 2

Designed and typeset by Martin Bristow

Printed in the United States of America by Quebecor World,
Martinsburg, WV

CONTENTS

In memory of my father, Alec Morton,
and for the people of Somerset County,
Pennsylvania, and especially the miners, their
families, and the rescue workers

I waited patiently for the Lord;
He turned to me and heard my cry.
He lifted me out of the slimy pit,
Out of the mud and mire;
He set my feet on a rock
And gave me a firm place to stand.

PSALM 40: 1–2 (New International Version)

PREFACE AND ACKNOWLEDGMENTS

ON HALLOWED GROUND

'WE BELIEVE IN HEROES.'

THIS SIMPLE and, in the circumstances, poignant sentiment, scrawled on a flat piece of rock in a woodland clearing near the town of Shanksville, Pennsylvania, spoke volumes about the mood in America, post-11 September 2001. The unknown visitor had come to view the scene where the doomed United Airlines Flight 93 had plunged to earth, killing the al-Qaeda hijackers and the passengers and crew who had fought back against the terrorists, thereby preventing an even more terrible atrocity. There were no survivors. From that fateful September day the rallying cry 'Let's roll!' – the final words, heard over a cell phone, of passenger Todd Beamer, who joined others in tackling the hijackers – have come to symbolize the nation's resolute defiance in the face of calculated evil.

Just ten months later and not much over ten miles away, another rallying cry galvanized the country and the watching world. 'Nine for nine,' intoned Pennsylvania's Governor Mark Schweiker, as desperate efforts were made by hundreds of rescue workers to free nine miners who had been trapped below ground for days. In a world made darker since the 11 September atrocities, the success of this race against time and rising floodwaters to save men buried alive was, to America, uplifting, even miraculous, while the skill and determination of the rescuers was matched only by the stoical courage of the trapped miners.

Like millions of others around the world, I watched the TV transfixed as one by one these nine men, wearing the same look of startled bewilderment as newborn babies, were pulled from the depths of the earth. While the nine men were hailed, rightly, as heroes, I was as intrigued by the incredible story behind the making of their great escape. This was as much a triumph of human ingenuity as it was a tribute to the will to survive. As an aficionado of real-life adventure stories, I felt that the miners' story in some ways resembled the true story of the fate of a New England fishing crew, described in Sebastian Junger's book, subsequently a movie, *The Perfect Storm*. Only, this time, the elemental encounter between fragile man and the unforgiving forces of nature had a happy ending.

Here then was a chance to piece together an account of a remarkable true-life drama that had not only gripped the imagination of the millions of people who saw it played out on television, but also, in a world clouded by calamity and hatred, was in itself a celebration of the best in the human spirit. Just forty-eight hours after the men were pulled to the surface, I found myself in Somerset County, sixty miles or so south-east of Pittsburgh, watching workers clearing up at the site of the rescue. I quickly discovered that, for once, the word 'miracle' – so beloved of, and overused by, the media – was no exaggeration. With a deep farmer's pond filled with slime-green water on one side, a main road and a cemetery on the other, it seemed that some other hand had been at work in allowing the rescue to take place in a field the size of a baseball pitch. As the complex story unfolded, the confluence of circumstances appeared to be simply overwhelming. 'Everything that had to go right did go right, which is very rare in a rescue,' remarked one engineer.

Beyond that, however, rescuers and rescued alike believed that the men's deliverance was destined, that it was as much about faith as physics. It is little wonder, therefore, that the field where the rescue took place has come to be viewed as hallowed ground, attracting a steady stream of the curious and the pious. They come to look and reflect on a miracle before driving ten miles east to Shanksville, to the site where Flight 93 crashed, leaving more than forty people dead, almost all of them innocent passengers and crew.

Yet the story of the rescue of the men from the Quecreek Number 1 mine is more than just a meditation on metaphysics. It is also a testament to teamwork, comradeship and unbidden generosity, as total strangers went to the aid of others not simply because it was their job to do so, but because they felt an innate kinship with the men trapped below. When farmer Bill Arnold was told that he had miners trapped beneath his property his first and immediate reaction was to open up his land to the engineers and drillers. 'Level my house if you have to – anything to get them out,' he volunteered. Many others echoed that selfless spirit during the hours and days of the rescue. The fact that volunteers served 4,375 meals, 7,000 snacks, 9,000 cups of coffee and 25,000 cold drinks in those few days, is testimony to the numbers who gave their time, energy and effort, often for no reward.

For everyone, it was an intense and emotionally draining experience, joy and anxiety existing side by side; several described it as almost akin to the tangle of feelings experienced at the birth of a child. That rawness was reflected in the interviews I conducted as people relived in words a period in their lives that none will ever forget. For most, particularly family, friends and rescuers, describing the moment when they heard that the men were alive brought tears or, at the very least, a lengthy pause while they gathered themselves to renew the absorbing narrative of their part in a story that, for many, has renewed their faith in human nature. Others, like miner Ron

Schad, broke down, reliving his personal nightmare underground as he spoke of his desperate efforts to escape the gushing waters.

It was both a privilege and a humbling experience to speak to those who were intimately involved in this drama. For a time, it enthralled the world, yet, for all the publicity, for the most part they were modest and self-effacing about their own roles, while open and honest about the tremendous difficulties they faced. On a personal note, a few weeks before the drama at Quecreek, my own father died after a long illness. To be admitted, however briefly, into the circle of people who gave of themselves so selflessly in order to assist others, helped me to cope with his loss, and I thank them for that.

I am grateful, too, for the tremendous help I received in Pennsylvania from many of the people involved; the parts they played are to be found in the narrative. In particular I would like to thank: Gerry Davis, Dr Jeffery Kravitz, Assistant Secretary of Labor Dave Lauriski, Amy Louviere, Kevin Stricklin, Joe Tortorea and John Urosek from the Mine Safety and Health Administration, US Department of Labor; Dr Richard Kunkle and Danny Sacco from the Special Medical Response Team; Bill and Lori Arnold, the Reverend Joseph Beer, Father Martin Breski, Eric Brant, Michael Brant, Barry Carlson, Doug and Cathy Custer, Mike Drewecki, Kathy Engle, Bill, Rona and Brock Hemminger, Tom Hoffman, Joe Kostyk, Julie Marker, Jim Mayak, Gerry Mills, Father Jack O'Malley, Dave, Ryan and Kathy Petree, Andrea Policicchio, Ron and Diana Schad, Karen Schafer, Eric Spiker, Katharine Snyder, Larry Summerville, John Weir, land manager for PBS Coal, Mark and Robin Zambanini. Those among them who lent or obtained photographs are also acknowledged elsewhere. I hope I have understood and explained the many complexities of the story, but if I have failed at any point, the fault is mine, rather than that of those who gave unstintingly of their advice and time.

I would also like to thank my American researchers, Angie Brant and Carmen DiCiccio, for working so hard under such pressure, as well as Darlene Marsh and her team of transcribers in Johnstown, Pennsylvania, who came to my aid in the nick of time. I owe a particular debt to Michael O'Mara, my publisher of sixteen years, who backed my hunch that this was a book worth writing, even though he had never heard of *The Perfect Storm*. I am, as ever, grateful to my editor, Toby Buchan, and to the editorial team at Michael O'Mara Books, especially Gabrielle Mander, Rhian McKay, Rod Green, Diana Briscoe and Judith Palmer. My thanks, too, to Glen Saville for his cover design, and to Martin Bristow for designing the text.

ANDREW MORTON
Somerset County, Pennsylvania and London,
July–September 2002

PHOTOGRAPH ACKNOWLEDGMENTS

Author: 2–3 main photo, 4–5 main photo, 4 top, 4 bottom,
 5 top, 5 center, 13 center, 15 top left, 16 top left inset,
 16 top center inset, 16 center inset, 16 top main photo;
Father Martin Breski: 2 top, 2 bottom right, 3 top right,
 3 center, 3 bottom left, 10 bottom right inset, 15 top right;
Commonwealth Media Services, Commonwealth of
 Pennsylvania: 6 top inset, 7 bottom left, 7 bottom right,
 8 top, 8 bottom, 9 bottom, 13 bottom;
Daily American, Somerset, PA: 2 bottom left, 3 top left;
Mine Safety and Health Administration, US Department of
 Labor: 3 bottom right, 6 main photo, 7 center right,
 12 bottom, 14 bottom, 16 bottom;
New Republic, Meyersdale, PA: 14 top;
PA Photos: 1, 7 top;
Reuters: 6 bottom inset, 9 top, 10 top, 10 center inset, 12 top,
 13 top, 15 bottom;
Ron Schad: 5 bottom left;
Special Medical Response Team: 10 bottom main photo,
 11 top, 11 bottom, 16 top right inset;
Betty Lou Wacko: 4 center, 5 bottom right

Chapter I

A DAY AT THE OFFICE WITH BIG JOE AND CO.

FROM HIS STAINED GRAY T-SHIRT and his black baseball cap emblazoned with a Harley-Davidson motorcycle motif, to the livid blue-and-red tattoos on his muscled upper arms, Dave Petree looks little different from countless other working men in America's heartland. In better shape, certainly. Even though he is in his late fifties, he has the sinuous, muscled physique of a man half his age. It is the walk that gives him away, though, the loose, rangy, rolling gait of a man who has spent most of his life crawling on his knees beneath a low roof, or angling his body against rough-hewn walls; a man used to taking his ease hundreds of feet underground, squatting on his upright hammer. Tough, uncompromising and straight as a die, Dave Petree comes from a mining family whose men have dug coal for decades.

For generations the Petree family, like many other Pennsylvania families, farmed the land, hunted in the woods and hewed the coal in Somerset County, a green country of lakes and forest some sixty miles to the south-east of Pittsburgh, Pennsylvania. Like the English county that is its namesake, Somerset was, and to a considerable extent remains, uncompromisingly rural, but blessed – some would say cursed – with abundant outcrops of coal lying so close to the surface that early settlers found that they could pick baskets of 'black gold'* as easily as ripe cherries.

Even in the 1950s when Dave Petree, aged just thirteen, first went to work full time in the family's modest mine, little had changed since those early days. True, the coal now had to be mined in underground workings, and while his father worked at the face with a pick and shovel, Dave helped around him, gathering coal, loading the wagon that would carry it back to the mine entrance and tending the rudimentary equipment. For the most part he took care of the family's pit pony, a docile animal that would stand patiently while her cart was loaded before being led out of the darkness. Every weekend they put the pony in the horse trailer, hitched it to the back of their car and drove her to a nearby farm. One of Dave's most vivid childhood memories is of seeing the transformation in that sturdy beast as soon as she was released into a field. It was like watching a different animal as she frisked and gamboled around the paddock. Come Sunday night they always had a tough time catching and loading her, but once she was in the trailer she would become quiet and biddable once more, stoically awaiting her fate – another week's work in the mine.

Doubtless she instinctively realized that mining was a dark, dirty and dangerous affair. Dave laughs at the memory of how he would hold up a piece of string so that his father, using a flashlight or a candle, whichever was handiest, could see how far into the coalface they had dug. It was by that hit-and-miss method that they drew up the maps which, one day, other miners might follow.

Just as cavalier was the macho disregard for safety. Even today, you will see miners wearing baseball caps embroidered with the legend, 'Mining: the second most dangerous profession'. Only

* Long before oil came to be known as 'black gold', the term was widely applied to coal in both Britain and the United States.

Alaskan crab fishermen fare worse, they will proudly tell you. The belief that, when underground, a miner ate the best part of his meal, the dessert, first because he didn't know if he would live long enough to eat more than one course, was not a legend, but a plain fact of life.

One day, after he had worked in commercial mines for a few years, Dave suffered an accident when he got himself caught between a piece of machinery and what miners call the 'rib' or wall of the mine. His steel-capped boots were crushed, severely injuring his feet, and he was carried out to the mine entrance and from there to a hastily summoned doctor who amputated his toes. 'Gave them back to me in a bag to keep,' he jokes. His wife Kathy shares his robust black humor, complaining that when he splays out, barefoot, in front of the TV, the stumps of his big toes obscure her view of the screen.

Dave's experience did not keep him from mining, nor has it put off their son, Ryan, known as 'Squirrel', from following in his father's footsteps. At 6 feet 3 inches he is tall for a miner, although that is no problem as far as he is concerned. 'I enjoy coal mining. I really do. It's in the family. It's in the blood,' he says. For the last nine years, since he left school at seventeen, he has worked down the mines. Even though the mine he works in is non-union, the money is good for the area – around $15 an hour, plus bonuses for safety and productivity. A lot better than flipping burgers or pumping gas, especially as he and his long-time girlfriend, Jessica, plan to marry soon.

Since March 2002 Ryan and his father had worked on the same crew for the same outfit, the Black Wolf Coal Company, which had recently opened a deep mine at Quecreek, a former mining-company village of around fifty houses founded in 1913 by Charles J. Harrison, a prominent local lawyer and business-man. Employing just sixty-three men, Quecreek Number 1 is a modest mine, turning out around 600,000 tons of coal a year, a drop in the bucket compared with the millions of tons produced by Consol Energy (as the Consolidation Coal Company is now known), the largest in Pennsylvania. Bounded by woodland and a couple of dairy farms, it is easier to pass the mine than to spot it. Until July 2002, its one tenuous claim to fame was that it was ultimately owned by PBS Mining, the company that owned the land at Shanksville, a few miles to the east, where Flight 93 crashed on 11 September 2001 after a group of passengers had attacked al-Qaeda terrorists, preventing them from using the airplane as a weapon to attack the nation's capital. The area is now a shrine to the heroism shown by the passengers and crew.

Not quite a year later, on the afternoon of Wednesday, 24 July 2002, as Ryan swung by his father's home in the mining town of Windber and picked him up for the thirty-five-minute ride to the mine, work was the last thing on their minds. With the NASCAR racing season in full swing – Dave supports Dodge – the talk was of that Sunday's Pennsylvania 500, which promised to be a real battle between Dodge's Sterling Martin and Chevrolet's Dale Earnhardt Jr and Jimmie Johnson. Inevitably, too, their talk also ranged over the coming hunting season, which would start in September, and their memories of past trips.

Not far behind them on Highway 219 were two other members of their crew, Joe Kostyk and Ron Schad. These two miners had only one thing in mind. While Joe drove them in his Ford Ranger pickup, he and Ron worked on their plans for a much-anticipated fishing trip that coming weekend. Life was looking good. The hunting season was due to start, the Pittsburgh Steelers football team was limbering up for their NFL opener in a few weeks, and a fishing trip beckoned. 'We could not wait for quitting time and we could not believe it was only Wednesday,' recalls Ron. Two weeks earlier he had gone on another fishing trip to the Juniata River with a good friend from the parallel crew, Tom Foy, known by everyone as 'Tucker' because, like the nursery-rhyme character Tommy Tucker, he was short and round and always hungry.

Mention fishing to Ron and his gray-green eyes light up. That morning he had carefully assembled the gear that he and Joe, his next-door neighbor, would take with them, the only debate being about whose boat to use. Indeed, the basement den of Ron's home in the former mining community of Salix is a memorial to the great outdoors. On display are antlers, turkey feathers and mounted steelhead trout from hunting and fishing trips gone by, as well as a veritable arsenal of hunting rifles and an array of top-of-the-line fishing tackle.

Also on display in the den is a signed photograph of the presidential helicopter, *Marine One*, dating from the days in the 1970s when Ron had been a member of the US Marines helicopter guard for the late President Nixon. The highlight of his two-year stint with the President was an official trip to the Bahamas where on his days off – inevitably – he went fishing. Of course, there was also the small matter of meeting his future wife, Diana, who at the time worked for the FBI's Missing Persons section. It was an attraction of opposites: she an outspoken, if conservative, city girl from Texas, he a softly spoken farm boy from Somerset County, Pennsylvania. In those days, however, Ron was something of a rowdy. Married to him for thirty years, Diana still remembers the day he arrived on a date sporting a black eye after a barroom rumble. 'Oh, he was a badass,' she says with a smile. Now forty-nine, the only rumble Ron cares for today is the splashing of a hard-fighting fish at the end of his line.

While Ron was sorting out the tackle, Joe – known as 'Big Joe', as much for his obdurate nature as for his physique – was cooking spaghetti for his wife, Andrea, and three children, so that their meal would be ready when she returned home from her government job. He likes cooking, and it was one way of keeping in touch with his family. When he was on the four-to-eleven shift he saw little enough of them; they were in bed when he got home, and had gone to work or to school before he woke. With the cooking finished, he chewed over problems with the contractors who were building a bedroom extension on to his home. Then at half-past two, as normal, he called on Ron to hitch a ride to work for the four-o'clock shift.

Something was niggling Leslie Mayhugh, and she didn't quite know what. Her friends had noticed that she was bothered by something, too. A couple of weeks before she had surprised her friends at the Beverly nursing home in Meyersdale, where she worked part time as a nurse, when she asked them about being baptized, a question that in turn led to a discussion of the after-life. Although Leslie, like almost everyone else she knew, believed in God, she never went to church and tended to shy away from religious talk. 'It was weird,' recalls Kathy Engle, who describes Leslie as the clown of a group of friends fondly known as 'The Network'. Kathy, who herself had been baptized in May 2002, told her friend that, knowing that some religious-minded people argue that you cannot go to Heaven unless you have been baptized, 'it was better to be safe than sorry'.

It was a conversation that stuck in the minds of everyone who was there, a casual chat that would soon come back to haunt them. At the time, the same thought struck them all: was this the same happy-go-lucky twenty-eight-year-old who had blown $400 during a gambling trip to Atlantic City? The one who had a happy knack of snagging the $1,100 jackpot at her Tuesday-night bingo sessions, and who always seemed to come out ahead on the weekly lottery? Most important in the good-for-tune stakes, she had a husband who religiously handed over his paycheck and told her, 'Spend it on what you like.'

As far as her friends were concerned, Leslie had also drawn a winning ticket in the lottery of life, with the perfect marriage, a husband who adored her, and two lovely children, Kelsey and Tyler. Indeed, when she had first started dating Harry Blaine Mayhugh – affectionately known as 'Stinky' – in her junior year at Meyersdale High School, she had been the envy of all her friends. The local pin-up, Blaine – he hates the name Harry – had just left the same school, where he had played for the football and baseball teams. 'Threw the best curveball I've ever seen,' says former classmate Michael Brant, admiringly. It was no surprise that the teenager, voted 'Most Daring' by his schoolfriends and who bequeathed his hunting skills to his teachers in a fake 'will' in his school yearbook, should decide to enroll in the US Navy, where it was his ambition to become a member of one of the USN's elite special-forces units, the Navy SEALs (Sea-Air-Land).

He may have broken a few hearts, but it was no surprise, either, when, two years after they began courting, Blaine and Leslie married before a Justice of the Peace while he was on leave from the Navy. 'They are absolute lovebirds, they were made for each other,' observes another member of 'The Network', thirty-four-year-old Karen Schaffer. 'They know what each other is thinking, like they have the same brain.'

In fact, leaving Leslie behind was one of the main reasons why the Navy didn't work out for Blaine. In 1992, having completed two years' service, he left the Navy and for a short while took a job in a factory before working for a lawn-care contractor. In 1997, enticed by the prospect of earning decent money, he became a 'red hat', as trainee miners are known.

It was not a prospect that thrilled his mother, Margie, or his father Harry Blaine Sr, a retired miner who had worked in open mines. They had seen the heart ripped out of too many families by mine accidents. Even though Leslie was from a mining family – her father, Tom 'Tucker' Foy, had been a miner since before she was born – she was always uneasy about the inherent dangers of the job. At least, she confided to close friends, if anything should ever happen to Blaine – which God forbid – her eight-year-old son, Tyler, would still have his grandpa Tucker left to take him on the fishing and hunting trips his father would normally have organized.

When Blaine left for the mine each day, Leslie joined that wide community of women, the wives of fishermen, oil-rig workers, miners and others, who can never quite be certain whether their men will ever come home again. Although only rarely articulated, that uncertainty was always there, rooted deep in the back of her mind. Every day during their ten years of marriage she had been there to kiss him farewell, and every night she waited up – often until after midnight – until he was safely home. Blaine was the same. He would wait up for her when she was on the late shift at the nursing home. As often as not, when the phone rang in the nurses' room late in the evening, when the girls were writing up their notes or just chatting among themselves, it would be Blaine calling to ask when his wife would be coming home. In his heart he didn't want Leslie to work, while she would have been a whole lot happier if he had worked at something, anything, other than mining. But in Meyersdale there aren't too many jobs paying $15 an hour plus bonuses.

Still, it was a comfort to Leslie that Blaine was working with her father on the same shift – three to eleven – and in the same crew at Quecreek mine. A close-knit family, she, Blaine and her parents, Tucker and Denise, were planning a camping trip in early August to celebrate their respective tenth and thirtieth wedding anniversaries. When Blaine left for work on 24 July she was tidying the house and yard in anticipation of their trip, mowing the grass at the bottom of the garden. For once she waved him a cheery goodbye, rather than giving him a kiss. 'See you later,' she called as he drove off.

In fact, on that fateful Wednesday Leslie was much more concerned about her father than her husband. Just four years before Tucker, now fifty-two and grandfather to seven children, had suffered a heart attack, undergoing angioplasty to open up clogged arteries and giving up drinking on doctor's orders. A couple of weeks earlier he had not been feeling too great, and his medication was changed after a visit to his doctor. Yet

24

although his wife Denise, who works as a cook, and four daughters had concerns about his health, Tucker just smiled and kept on going. 'I spent eighteen months in Vietnam and if I can live through that I can live through anything,' the former serviceman is fond of saying in his quick-fire drawl.

Like most miners that day, Tucker Foy had two things on his mind as he drove to Quecreek – the start of the hunting season, and that Sunday's Pennsylvania 500 NASCAR race. A locally famous hunter, Foy boasts that he can down a nine-point deer (which in Britain would be called an eighteen-pointer) with a single shot, attributing his prowess to having been brought up in a family of nine boys, spending his childhood roaming the woods and fields in pursuit of groundhogs, wild turkey and deer. As for NASCAR, he is not just an armchair fan. On one occasion he and a group of friends traveled to North Carolina to watch his favored Chevy team in action; 'One of the best weekends I ever had,' he says, with a chuckle of remembrance.

'Hi guys,' said Doug Custer as he walked into the lamp room at Quecreek mine, where his fellow miners were changing ready for the four-to-twelve shift. 'Who got laid last night?' His question brought a rueful collective shake of the head from the eight other men as they stripped off their jeans and T-shirts and climbed into what they call their 'rags' – long johns, shirts, socks and blue company overalls. For his part Doug, who has been a miner for more than twenty years, had spent that morning sealing his drive ready for the winter, his wife Cathy, a hospice nurse, having left for work at around six in the morning.

As he looked round the cramped room, a former portable office, he eased into the banter and joshing, the miners sipping coffee as they changed, moaning about the aches and pains of a demanding job. 'My knee won't take another day of this,' complained someone between slurps of coffee. 'What about my back?' grouched another. They rag each other remorselessly, savoring the easy but tightly knit brotherhood of men bonded to each other and to the earth, sharing the perils and the patter. For them mining is more than a job – it is a way of life. As Joe Kostyk observed, 'Miners grow into a good tight group. You have to. You have to look out for one another. When you are underground, you have eight or nine guys watch your back. That's what it takes or none of us are going to make it.' Everyone in the lamp room knew that, as had many of their fathers and grandfathers before them. That sense of shared experience, of mutual enterprise, of belonging, is, as the psychologist Anthony Clare argues, one of the secrets of happiness and fulfillment. While the miners themselves would almost certainly scoff at the high-flown language, they would agree with the sentiments.

Nevertheless, the price of becoming a member of that community of coal is high. Barry Carlson is a good example. Now a grandfather himself, he has been in the mines for thirty-eight years, since he was nineteen. He followed in his father's footsteps, starting on the same day as his brother Robert who, years later, was fatally electrocuted while underground.

Then there is Larry Summerville, who started in the mines thirty-three years ago, just a month after his father, also a miner, suffered a crippling spinal-cord injury. Larry, together with Dave Petree and his son Ryan, Ron Schad, Joe Kostyk, Barry Carlson, and Doug Custer, as well as Wendell Horner and acting fire boss Frank Stewart, a steady, reliable miner who lived outside the county, made up the nine members of the fateful four-o'clock shift at Quecreek mine.

An hour earlier, Blaine 'Stinky' Mayhugh and his father-in-law, Tom 'Tucker' Foy, had joined the rest of their crew for the three-o'clock shift. They were known as the loud ones of the bunch, Blaine always wisecracking and goofing around, Tucker talking nineteen to the dozen, teasing the other miners. 'He can make fun of a guy but he always laughs with you rather than against you,' recalls another Quecreek miner, Gerry Mills, who has worked with most of the men who were on the two shifts that afternoon.

While Tucker and Stinky were the jokers in the pack, crew chief Randy Fogle was the undisputed leader, respected for his common sense, hard work and dedication to the job. He is a reassuring, almost familiar, figure, often dressed in army fatigues, a plug of chewing tobacco in his mouth. Like most miners, Fogle is addicted to chewing tobacco and snuff, the men using these as substitutes for cigarettes, which are banned underground due to the risk of explosion. Naturally, as the crew chief, he likes to be in the center of the action, on and off duty. Former mine worker Jim Mayak remembers the occasion when Fogle brought his crew round to his house in Boswell and they all pitched in to put on a new roof, even though it was their day off. 'Randy carried bags of shingles on his shoulder all day. Never stopped,' recalls Mayak admiringly. 'He's that kind of guy, tough and hard-working.' Known variously as 'the Boss' or, by some of the younger miners – although never to his face – as 'Fat Fudge', Fogle has been around mines for most of his life. Little wonder. He lives in Garrett, an area known locally as 'Fogletown' where, inevitably, many of the families are related to one another; collectively, they have worked in the mines for a hundred years and more.

If Randy Fogle was the acknowledged leader, John Unger, known as 'Ung' or 'the Farmer', was the chaplain of the crew. With twenty-eight years of mining experience, the bespectacled, ruddy-faced fifty-two-year-old is well known far beyond the mining community. Large-hearted and instantly likable, Unger is a deeply committed Christian, active in the Maple Spring Church of Brethren church he attends near his Holspopple home. Like a number of local miners, he runs a small farm, known as Broken Down Acres, where he keeps thirty head of cattle on the eighty acres of pasture and crops. He is, too, plainly devoted to his wife Sue Ellen, who contracted multiple sclerosis fifteen years ago. Now only able to get around with the aid of a light-weight walker, Sue Ellen is affectionately nicknamed 'The Saint' for the quiet equanimity with which she copes with her crippling illness. In some ways it has served to strengthen their marriage and their faith. 'I love you, I adore you, I worship the ground beneath you,' John will often say to his partner of thirty years. Brock Hemminger, a twenty-one-year-old Marine who views John Unger as his surrogate father, says of him, 'He is a genuine Good Samaritan who helps people out, be they strangers or friends. The Ungers consider themselves down-home folk who work hard all week, have time for their family, have time for God and time to have fun at the weekends.'

The notion of fun for crew member Dennis Hall, nicknamed 'Harpo', is carving deer antlers and shaping them into handles for knives. With his curly gray hair and droopy Zapata-style moustache, Harpo is, as one of his coworkers noted, the epitome of the 'wild mountain man', a tough, independent – some would say cussed – character who yields to no man; the kind of man who would face down a grizzly bear if he had to. His love of mining is bone deep, and even the fact that he was trapped for an hour in a cave collapse at another mine in Somerset County, and later was smashed in the face by a drill that scarred him and broke his lower dentures, has not dimmed his enthusiasm. Ever since he started mining thirty years ago when he was nineteen, Harpo has always stood out from the crowd – a man's man in a man's world. In those days he wore his long, curly ginger hair tied back in a ponytail. 'When I first met him I thought, "What was that?"' remembers a fellow miner, Eric 'Spike' Spiker. 'But after we had worked together I got a lot of respect for him. He is quiet but dedicated to his job.'

Another modest member of the crew was fifty-year-old Robert 'Boogie' Pugh. When he arrived for work at around 2.15 on that Wednesday he had a lot on his mind. The weekend ahead was to be marked by a long-planned reunion of the Pugh family, and he and his girlfriend of many years, Cindy Thomas – Pugh's marriage ended in divorce eleven years ago – had been discussing last-minute details. Pugh relations were traveling from all over America for the celebration, and he had got up early that morning to replace a tatty carpet in his red-brick house in Boswell in preparation for the coming celebration. There was one thing he was sure about, however: he wasn't making any speeches.

Painfully shy, it is typical of him that he always sits in the back pew at the All Saints' Catholic church in Boswell where he and his family worship. Even though he has passed the necessary qualifications to become a fire boss (who is in charge of safety during a shift), Pugh, a miner for thirty-two years, has shied away from taking responsibility, preferring to continue looking after mine equipment. Respected by fellow miners for his quiet competence, Boogie, a former wrestling champion and center for the all-county football team, is also admired by local hunters for his uncanny ability to 'call' the wild turkeys he stalks. Most hunters use a mechanical caller to lure the birds within range of their guns.

One such admirer is another crew member, Ron Hileman, known as 'Hound Dog', an avid hunter and hiker who spends as much time as possible outdoors. A year younger than Pugh but educated in the same town, Hound Dog is a thirty-year veteran of the mines. From his home in Gray, where his wife runs the Little Kings and Queens day-care center, he had only a five-minute drive to get to the mine.

Also making up the nine-strong crew was John Phillippi, known as 'Flathead', who lives a couple of miles from Robert Pugh. Like Pugh, he was one of the quieter members of the group, content to leave Tucker, Stinky and the Boss to goof around. Even though his father is a retired miner, thirty-six-year-old Philippi, who has a son of twelve, went into mining more for the money than from a love of the work. As a coworker, Eric

Spiker, noted, 'Once you get the paycheck, you are hooked. You don't want to leave.'

As far as Mark 'Mo' Popernack was concerned, mining was in his blood, for the wiry, good-humored forty-one-year-old has followed in the footsteps of his father, Ed, a miner for most of his life. The Popernack men have a reputation as solid, hard-working miners, cool under pressure, and with a shrewd, if laid-back, approach to life. Married with two sons aged nine and ten, Mark, who has been mining for half his life, acknowledges that he is a different person when he is underground. 'It's difficult to explain,' he says, talking about the visceral, if largely unspoken, bond between miners. 'When I'm home with my wife and kids I'm a different person to when I'm in the mine. When I'm at work I'm focused on my job, digging coal. That's a different person to when you're at a park somewhere playing the rides with the kids.'

There was one member of the three-o'clock shift who was missing that day – apprentice miner Roger Schaffer Jr, who had taken his wife Lacey to an Ozzy Osbourne concert in Pittsburgh as a treat.

Had he been there, Schaffer would have joined in the routine grumbling in the lamp room that day as, like medieval knights preparing for battle, the nine-strong crew gingerly eased into their steel-capped rubber boots, and donned their self-rescuers – a breathing apparatus that theoretically gives a miner an hour of air in the event of fire or smoke – then their helmets, each with a detachable lamp connected to a battery pack that clips to the waist belt, and finally their kneepads. They were assigned to mine an area known as First Left, some 8,000 feet inside the mine and more than 200 feet below ground. The roof space there was low and it was wet as hell. To a man, the crew put on their heavy rubberized raincoats. Another Quecreek miner, Eric Grant, who was taking a shower at the end of his shift as the three-o'clock crew headed for the mine, observed, 'It was just another day at the office – water pouring from the roof and you finish up with a wet backside.' As far as he was concerned the job was simple: to mine as much coal as possible, as safely as possible; a view shared by most of his coworkers. At Quecreek, each shift will produce anything from 1,000 to 1,500 tons of coal, helping to hit the monthly target of, usually, around 55,000 tons – and a juicy production bonus for the miners.

Unlike many deep mines, where the coalface is reached by means of a vertical elevator that descends from the pithead, Quecreek is what's called a 'drive-in mine', approached through 'portals' driven into the hillside. The nine men of the three-to-eleven climbed into an old blue ambulance that took them down the ramp to the mouth of the mine. There they transferred to a mantrip, a low-slung, battery-powered four-wheeled transporter that went through the two airlocks near the mine entrance and on from there to the coalface about a mile and a half into the mine.

To an outsider the mine is a bewildering maze of crosscuts – the alleyways that run parallel to the face; travelways – the main highways to and from the face; beltways – the conveyor belts that transport the coal to the surface; and intake and out-take shafts, which ventilate the mine. Yet just as each miner could identify another simply by the pattern of reflective tape on his helmet, so they knew every rise and fall of the ground during the half-hour journey to the face. Had they needed to, they could probably have found their way back to the mine entrance blindfold.

In some ways, their work at the face reflected their outdoor pursuits. While they hunted and fished with buddies, the actual acts of stalking a deer or hooking and landing a fat trout are solitary, requiring individual skill and perseverance. Below ground they also worked as a team, but each man had a clearly defined job, which in turn meant that often they would barely pass a word to each other during the eight-hour shift. 'They were the elite miners, crews with two hundred years' experience between them,' noted Jim Mayak, a cousin of Bob Pugh's and a miner himself for twenty-eight years. 'They needed every ounce of that know-how as the mine was low and wet.'

When they reached the face, the foreman, Randy Fogle, performed numerous safety checks, testing for methane and other explosive or toxic gases, monitoring oxygen levels and testing the ventilation. This procedure usually takes about twenty minutes, and has to be completed to the foreman's satisfaction before the section can be powered up and work can begin.

Coal mining has come a long way from the days of sweating men hacking at the face with picks, while other men shoveled the coal away behind them. Today, the process is far more mechanized. Quecreek is a 'room-and-pillar' mine, which means that large 'rooms', about 4 feet high, are cut into the coal bed at right angles to the coalface, leaving behind a series of 'pillars' of coal and rock that support the roof and aid the flow of air. Each room in a section is about 20 feet wide, bounded on either side by pillars; these parallel rooms are crossed at regular intervals by crosscuts, so that, seen from above, the section shows a grid of rooms and crosscuts running between regularly spaced, equal-sized rectangular pillars. Cement-block walls are built between pillars from floor to roof to make air shafts running parallel to the rooms, the walls effectively sealing the shafts; the beltway also runs between pillars at right angles to the face. At the face there are numerous cuts where the remote-controlled continuous mining machine, or 'miner', a low-slung motorized device about eleven and a half feet wide with a rotating cutter head equipped with one hundred teeth, is set up to grind into the seam, breaking coal away from the face. It is controlled by the miner operator from a distance that keeps him safe from roof falls and debris, and churns out tons of coal, rock and rubble in minutes. This spews from the back of the machine on to a shuttle car, which takes the coal from the face to the conveyor belt.

The scoop, a small-scale digger, picks up spilt coal, cleans up the floor and pushes any rock dirt on to the roof and ribs (walls) to prevent the possibility of fire. As the miner grinds through the seam, roof bolters power into the roof and, every 4 feet, drop in plugs of resin and then attach long bolts to ensure against roof collapse, the most common cause of death and injury in coal mining. On this shift Mo Popernack and Flathead Phillippi worked together, the former operating the remote control for the continuous miner, the other carefully overseeing the water pipes for the machine's cooling system and the 995-volt electrical cable that powered the machine, while keeping a weather eye on the automatic methane monitor. Every twenty minutes they used a hand-held instrument to check the roof and ribs for the presence of combustible gases. Elsewhere, Ron Hileman and John Unger operated the roof bolters, Robert Pugh and Dennis Hall ran the coal shuttle, Blaine Mayhugh the scoop, with Tom Foy as the outby mechanic and Randy Fogle in overall charge, filling in where necessary.

The work on that shift was painfully slow going, with constant falls of gravelly rock making the extraction of coal time-consuming and messy. Even as Mo Popernack operated the miner slicing through what they called 'crud', he reflected that he couldn't wait for the weekend. They had been told that, because they were nearing the boundary between this face and the disused Saxman Number 2 mine, work would end here in a couple of days and they would move on to another section. By law they had to leave a 300-foot boundary between this section of the Quecreek mine and the abandoned Saxman working.

More than 2,000 feet away and 500 feet below them, the four-o'clock crew were faring little better. Their shift, in an area of the mine known as the Mains, had started slowly. First Ron Schad, the crew's mechanic, had to get a new battery for a faulty phone in their section, and then they got the slowest mantrip in the mine to take them to the face. They were working Entries Numbers 6 and 7, the lowest and wettest part of the mine. While the coal was good quality, the surrounding rock kept collapsing, giving the roof bolters, Dave Petree and Doug Custer, a hard time shoring up while Ryan Petree and Barry Carlson, who were operating the scoops, were kept busy by the tons of rubble falling from the roof. Joe Kostyk, the miner operator, remarks that 'A roof fall always makes you a little nervous but you know it's going to happen and you're ready for it. Sure when I first started I was really nervous but not so much now.' Halfway through the shift they moved to a new position. It was a little higher and a little drier which made loading the coal so much easier. 'It was an average day,' recalls Ron Schad. 'If you have a bad roof it is an average day. But nobody had gotten hurt.'

While Joe Kostyk and Mo Popernack were cursing the crud, 240 feet above them farmer Bill Arnold was counting his blessings. At eight o'clock that evening he and his father Melvin were baling the last of the day's hay. Even though his father is seventy-three and has officially retired five times, Bill has stopped trying to make him take things easy. That evening he was grateful for the help. His farm, which the family have owned since 1963, may look like a picture postcard, with its herd of 138 Friesian cattle, flock of wild Canada geese and angular red barns that make striking silhouettes at dusk, but it demands round-the-clock attention. It did not help that his energetic wife Lori was on the injured list, her ankle in plaster due to an inflamed tendon.

That Wednesday they had thirty acres of hay laying and it was just starting to be ready for baling. His son Benjamin, aged thirteen, was hard at work raking and 'tedding' (fluffing) the hay, and by nightfall they had forty bales finished. Bill, a stocky thirty-eight-year-old, remembers, 'I thought: "Boy, the rest will be just great for tomorrow.'" Just to make sure he went out when it was dark and started baling in Cemetery Field, adjacent to the graveyard of the Casebeer Lutheran church a couple of hundred yards from their farmhouse.

As a result, Bill missed eating a roast-pork supper that evening with his wife, sister-in-law Nikki and his four children. So he did not hear the youngest of his brood, Morgan, just three, say grace. Morgan thanked the Lord for the meal and for the nice trees, and prayed for big puddles to splash in.

He especially prayed for big puddles.

Chapter II

THE PRICE OF COAL

THE TWO MEN froze in alarm, their cap lamps highlighting the fear on their faces. Something was wrong. They had been miners long enough to know the meaning of every noise underground, and what it might presage. Later they would describe the sound from a nearby mined-out chamber as having been like a 'sharp popping' and a 'distant pistol shot.' They yelled for their shift boss to come and take a look. At that moment the roof gave way, a deafening, roaring torrent of water exploding into mine. 'It sounded like thunder, water poured down like Niagara Falls,' the overseer would later recall.

In mounting panic the three men sprinted up the slope towards the mine entrance, the raging waters lapping at their heels. Desperate to warn their comrades working deeper in the mine, they raised the alarm the moment they reached safety. The mine superintendent ordered the immediate evacuation of the entire mine.

The warning came too late for three other miners working in the section where the water broke through. With unbelievable force the flood thundered into the shaft at a rate of 2.7 million gallons per minute, overpowering them instantly, the men battered, crushed and drowned almost before they realized what was happening. In other parts of the mine, nine other miners faced the terror of a cold and miserable death, entombed in the darkness, some entirely alone, some with a workmate to share their last moments, all feeling the icy water inching inexorably higher. They clung to the tunnel roofs as the rising water displaced the ever more fetid air, frantically sucking in their last breaths before slipping beneath the surface.

As millions of gallons of water flooded into the May shaft, men waded chest high through the torrent, desperate to reach the elevators that would haul them to the surface. They came out a few at a time, and even when it seemed to the families and off-duty mine workers waiting despairingly at the pit head that all hope was gone, still more men would appear, greeted with tears from their loved ones and ragged cheers from spectators. One group of twenty-seven men spent seven hours battling through flooded tunnels to reach an abandoned air shaft that eventually led them to safety.

Amid the tragedy, the courage of Italian miner Amedeo Pancotti stood out. He led one group to safety, digging through 30 feet of debris before climbing a 50-foot wall to the surface, where he went for help. The actions of other miners like Joe Stella, who led six men to safety through an abandoned air shaft, and foreman Myron Thomas, who ensured the survival of his crew, were later celebrated in song and poetry.

For the morning of 22 January 1959, when the mighty Susquehanna River poured into the Knox Coal Company's Port Griffith mine in Pennsylvania, changed the face of coal mining in America for ever. Of the eighty-one men who entered the mine that day, only sixty-nine lived to tell the harrowing story of life and death in the rapidly flooding mine. The bodies of the missing twelve were never recovered.

For three days rescuers poured everything into the surging river to stem the flow. The awesome sight of nearly a hundred railroad cars, as well as chunks of ice as big as houses, being swallowed, like so many bath toys, by the swirling vortex as it flowed into the mine during that bitter January overwhelmed many of those who witnessed it.

An investigation into the disaster eventually unraveled a cynical conspiracy of greed, racketeering and corruption. The mine owners, aided by ineffectual mine inspectors and figures from the world of organized crime, had tried to grab every last ton of anthracite coal lying under the river. Miners had unknowingly cut to within 6 feet of the river bed, whereas the minimum legal thickness of rock for a tunnel roof was 35 feet. In their lust for 'black diamonds' (as coal was sometimes known), the owners had gambled with the lives of their miners. Yet although so many men paid the full price, few of the culprits were ever brought to justice. True, the tragedy did lead, years later, to a change in the safety laws, but the immediate impact of the Knox disaster was effectively to end underground mining in this corner of Pennsylvania, throwing thousands of men out of work and turning Port Griffith into a ghost town.

Every year since, a ceremony of remembrance has been held at Port Griffith as, more than forty years later, families recall those terrible January days. Audrey Calvey, whose father, John Baloga, was one of the twelve victims, has never stopped thinking about his last moments alive. 'It bothers me,' she says. 'I wonder where his body is, how long did he suffer, how long did it take the water to reach the top.'

While mine inundations have been rare in the bloody history of American coal mining, this has not diminished the grief, anguish and loss that follow in the wake of such disasters. The gaggle of sobbing women and frightened children waiting at the pithead in the mining town of Coaldale in Panther Valley, Pennsylvania, must have experienced dreadful thoughts similar to those of Audrey Calvey as they awaited news of their loved ones. On Monday, 27 September 1915, there were few in the mining town who held out much hope for the survival of eleven miners trapped after water burst into the mine.

When rescue teams ventured into the mine the sight that greeted them was devastating. Fallen timbers, mud, smashed machinery and loose coal, together with the presence of 'black damp' – a highly dangerous, suffocating gas – made the trapped miners' chances of survival slim indeed. The local newspaper reflected the mood of despondency. 'Fears expressed that entombed men may not be reached alive,' ran the headline on the second day of the drama. There had been no tapping on the walls or roof, no cries for help from inside the mine. The interior was as silent as the grave.

Remarkably, on the second day following the inundation, two of those trapped and feared lost, William 'Kaska Bill' Watkins and George 'Gint' Hollywood, were rescued near the surface. It brought the 150 rescuers renewed hope as they worked feverishly to find the remaining men. Twenty-four hours later there was much joy as a third miner, William 'Kelly' Watkins, was able to walk unaided from the mine. According to contemporary accounts, he coolly sent a message to his wife informing her that he was in good shape and would be coming home for supper. The fate of the remaining eight, though, was unknown.

Incredibly, after surviving six days without food and with only floodwater to drink, the eight missing men were discovered alive. On 3 October, once the water had receded and the mass of debris been cleared, foreman John Humphries ventured down the mine shaft, shouting as he went. His call was returned by Elmer Herring, the strongest of those entombed, who was still trapped behind fallen rubble. His first words were hardly historic or grateful. 'My God, man, turn your light the other way, it is blinding me,' he yelled. When Humphries asked about the other men, he was told that they were all alive. The foreman found them huddled together for warmth and company.

As the men were taken to the surface, a huge crowd of onlookers, members of the miners' families, rescuers and townsfolk greeted them as they emerged, blinking in the sunlight. Everyone agreed that they were witnessing a real-life miracle, particularly as none of the men was badly injured. 'They survived hardships which cannot be pictured by tongue or pen,' wrote the editor of the local paper.

To aid their recovery, the local surgeon gave them all mugs of hot coffee and an injection to stimulate their weakened hearts. They spent several days in Coaldale hospital and then, dressed in new black suits, posed for a local photographer before going home to their wives and families. They were paid a consideration shift of $3.33 – the equivalent of eight hours' pay – to compensate them for their ordeal. After a few days' recuperation, all went back to the mine. The remarkable parallels with the events that were to take place at Quecreek eighty-seven years later are inescapable.

Ironically, it is not water, but fire, explosions and roof collapses that miners fear the most. With good reason, as these have caused the majority of the 104,000 recorded deaths in US mining since 1900. Inevitably, since Pennsylvania was the first home of coal mining in the United States, the price of coal in this state has been particularly high, paid in broken bodies, ruined lives and grieving families. At the turn of the last century, an average of 1,000 men died in Pennsylvania's coal mines every year, or roughly 3 deaths for every day of the year. The darkest year was 1907, when mining in the state resulted in 1,514 fatalities. That year also saw the state's worst ever mine disaster when, on 19 December, some 239 men were killed at the Pittsburgh Coal Company's Darr Mine in Westmoreland County.

Situated on the Youghiogheny River near Van Meter, the Darr pit drew its miners from surrounding towns like Wickhaven and Jacob's Creek, in the adjacent Lafayette County. That morning their wives and families, off-duty miners and townsfolk needed no wailing pit siren to tell them that something had gone terribly wrong. It felt as though there had been an earth-quake, the ground underfoot shuddering and houses on both sides of the river shaking. In fact, the earthquake was man-made, the result of a massive explosion ripping through the mine. No one below ground at Darr stood a chance of survival.

Men tunneling two miles inside the mine had encountered a pocket of methane gas. The gas, which occurs naturally in coal mines, had combined with the coal dust and oxygen in the underground atmosphere to produce a mixture that was both highly explosive and extremely volatile. At that time mine work-ers used lamps with an open flame. The men underground at Darr never stood a chance. The flames ignited the gas, resulting in a massive explosion and a searing fireball that scorched through the tunnels.

Once the ensuing fire had been extinguished, rescuers entered the mine on what they knew would be a grisly opera-tion to recover bodies. Their fears were amply justified. The first team into the mine was reported to have got as far as the pit boss's underground office, still almost a mile from the coal-face, where they found five bodies, one of which had been decapitated. Contemporary newspaper reports described the scenes of carnage as mangled and charred bodies were recov-ered and taken to a large tent that had been set up on the site as a temporary morgue.

The Pennsylvania tragedy came less than two weeks after America's worst ever mining disaster, which happened not many miles away in neighboring West Virginia. On the morning of 6 December at the Consolidation Coal Company's Monongah Mine near Fairmont, around 380 men and boys had just begun their shift in mines Number Six and Number Eight when a 'shocking' explosion rocked the entire area. Again it was believed that explosive gas ignited by open-flame lamps caused the inferno. The blast completely wrecked the mine workings, caus-ing an enormous cave-in that trapped 360 miners underground, although many of these had been killed outright. A twelve-year-old boy worker was also killed at the surface.

Over the next two days rescue efforts were hampered when fires broke out in both mine workings. Even so, there could have been little hope for those under the ground. In the bitter cold, friends and family kept vigil at the mine entrance, waiting anxiously for news, and praying for a miracle that never came. The Monongah disaster killed 362 men, widowed 250 women, and left more than 1,000 children fatherless. Ironically, many of those children would be forced to help support their families by taking jobs in the mines.

While it was the major disasters which made the headlines, the day-to-day rhythm of mining was brutal and bloody, where sudden death or crippling injury was an ever-present threat. In the nineteenth and early twentieth centuries, with few safety laws and no unions, mine owners and the press of the day invariably blamed any accident on the miners themselves. Thus the myth of the 'careless miner' was born. When their men set off for a shift, miners' wives never knew whether they would return alive. This enduring uncertainty was symbolized by the 'Black Maria', a horse-drawn (later motorized) wagon that was used to carry severely injured miners home from the pit. Its arrival in a locality would strike terror into the hearts of the wives there, and women would stand on the front porches or stoops to watch it pass, hoping that it would not stop at their home. If the miner was dead, his body would be taken from the Black Maria and placed in the porch of his home. If he were fatally injured, he would be left for his wife to care for, so that his last few hours might be as comfortable as possible.

In those days, the coal company's responsibility ended at the miner's front door. The bereaved family, now without its main breadwinner, would simply be left to fend for itself. While one consequence of this was that it forced miners' children underground in order to provide for their families, another was that it forged a community notable for its solidarity and fierce loyalty. While workers in other industries, notably commercial fishing, suffered equal privation and hardship, there can be few other walks of life in which communities of families survived, side-by-side in such an atmosphere of shared adversity, and fewer still where the workers form the bond of brotherhood that exists to this day between those who labor underground.

While the coal companies were quick to wash their hands of miners who were no longer of use, they worked assiduously to control the lives of their employees, viciously fighting any attempts at unionization and settling miners in company towns where the word of the boss was law. In Somerset County, one such town, Gray, was established in 1913 by the Consolidation Coal Company. The town reputedly took its name from the color used to paint the company houses. No longer a company town, Gray is still home to a number of miners, including Ronald Hileman, who was on the three-o'clock shift at Quecreek one Wednesday in July 2002.

During World War I, over 375,000 people were employed by the coal operators in Pennsylvania, and the well-being of the miners' families was almost entirely reliant on the coal companies. In those early days a typical miner's home – which he rented from the company – would have just four rooms, with no inside plumbing or running water, although some did have electric light. Household necessities would be purchased from a company-owned store, usually at huge mark-ups. Besides fresh milk, eggs, meat and cloth for the family's clothes, the miner had to buy all of the tools he required for his job from the store – even the oil for his lamp. The company also sold the miner the coal he needed to heat his home and, if there was a local doctor, he would have to pay a monthly fee to cover his family's medical expenses.

Everything bought from the company in this way would be charged to an account – often through the use of 'scrip', the company's own paper money or metal coinage – and deducted from the miner's wages via a system known as 'check off'. The popular 1950s hit 'Sixteen Tons', which contained the line 'I owe my soul to the company store', summed up the feelings of underpaid miners.

It was not uncommon for them to have no wages left at all on payday because of all the deductions. In order to reduce their dependence on this industrial version of legalized slavery, most turned whatever backyard they had into vegetable gardens, and those who could would go hunting or fishing whenever the opportunity presented itself.

In spite of the obvious dangers of the profession, economic hardship, as well as accidents, often forced families to send their sons to join their fathers in the mines. Far from being reluctant, however, the sons were most often proud to be following in their fathers' footsteps. Mining, especially in Pennsylvania, is a family affair. It is not unusual for miners to be the sons of miners who were, in turn, themselves the sons of miners. Mining is often said to be 'in the blood', and miners describe the only thing worse than being a miner as being an unemployed miner. Of the eighteen men who went down the mine at Quecreek on Wednesday, 26 July 2002, the majority were from mining families, and most had learned about the job at their grandfather's knee. Indeed, miners nowadays are something of an elite group, and landing work in the mines, where wages can be substantially higher than for other forms of manual labor, often comes down to 'knowing somebody in the job'. Inevitably, this perpetuates the family tradition.

Pennsylvania's mining communities today, however, are nowhere near as densely populated as they were when miners and their families lived shoulder to shoulder in the company towns. As late as 1979 there were 60,000 miners in the state. Now there are fewer than 10,000, with just over 900 of Somerset County's population of 80,000 employed in mining.

Yet coal output in the United States has doubled in the last 70 years, rising from 564 million tons in 1923 to over 1,100 million last year. Furthermore, substantial changes in the law, notably the creation, in 1973, of the Mining Enforcement and Safety Adminstration within the US Department of the Interior, which in 1977 became the Mine Safety and Health Administration and transferred to the US Department of Labor, have improved safety immeasurably.

Three decades ago, some 150 coal miners were killed each year in the United States. Now that figure is around forty, although it is a rare miner who does not have his own story of an injury or narrow escape underground. Local Somerset miner Charlie Stufft, now retired, knows several men who lost their arms, one who lost four fingers on one hand, and a neighbor who almost had his nose ripped off. He is the first to agree that, while technology has made a difference, it has not made mines safe places. Mining is hardly the profession that most middle-class parents dream of for their children.

Despite the introduction of ever more sophisticated mining machinery, the men (and, nowadays, women) who mine coal, share a physically demanding task, working in conditions which people who are used to air-conditioned offices and ergonomically engineered workstations would find intolerable. (Paradoxically, many miners who have tried working in light and spacious offices find such jobs unsatisfying.) Mining, however, is more than just a job; it is a way of life, one that involves a communal lifestyle whose values and operations hark back to a different era, a world incomprehensible to the soft-handed sons and daughters of the computer era. While the grinding poverty and exploitation of miners has gone – at least in America – the spirit that unites mine workers is as strong today as ever it was. As syndicated newspaper columnist Llewellyn King observes, 'Miners love to mine. They are caught up in the manliness of it, the romance of it, and the permanence of working underground.

The dying trades of fishing, steel-making and mining have about them an aura of big men doing big work in extreme conditions.'

The shared dangers, the bonds of trust and comradeship, create a deeply masculine community of endeavor which, while it may be short on speeches, is long on action. Firm in their faith, loyal to their country, suspicious of outsiders and wary of cities, their insularity encourages that solidarity. Working underground and isolated from everyday life, they are literally a breed apart. John Weir, the land manager for PBS Coal, which leases the mining rights for the Quecreek mine to the Black Wolf Company, has been around miners all his life. They are a different race, he says, adding: 'When they aren't in the mine, they talk about mining and, when they are in the mine, they lie about women and hunting.'

Indeed, hunting is in their blood almost as much as mining. The men who work together underground invariably spend their free time together as well, usually hunting and fishing. The great outdoors satisfies their desire for physical activity and freedom from the cares of everyday life that mining also gives them. Mining is therefore as much an escape as hunting, men losing themselves in the rhythms of the job, be it working a new seam or stalking a deer.

Just as the hunter relies on his individual prowess to succeed, so a miner often works alone underground, separated from his coworkers, reliant only on his skills. All of this serves to reinforce the enduring, somewhat romantic image of the miner as an individual of great strength of character, as devoted to his fellow miners as he is to his family, existing within a community where the families stand steadfast behind their men.

It was these rich and abundant coal seams that drew immigrants from all over Europe to Pennsylvania. In 1681, William Penn, the London-born son of an admiral, was granted the land and the right to establish a British colony in the region by King

Charles II. Ironically the sovereign – whose thirteenth-century ancestor, King Edward I, imposed the death penalty for burning coal as he believed it gave off 'poisonous odors' – was handing Penn what has been described as the world's most valuable mineral deposit, containing an estimated 107 billion tons of coal. It was not until years after Penn's death in 1752, however, that men began mining, hewing coal from the hills around Fort Pitt, the settlement that would later become Pittsburgh.

One of Penn's main purposes in establishing the colony was to provide a home for a persecuted religious sect of which he was a supporter, namely the Society of Friends, commonly known as the Quakers. In Pennsylvania, William Penn provided them with a safe haven in which to practice their religion unmolested. The same basic right was afforded to other immigrants and settlers, including the Amish, the Mennonites, Swedish Lutherans, and Germans who brought with them the Reformed Church and settled as Baptist Brethren.

As a result, the colony quickly gained a reputation as a tolerant, multi-cultural society. The Quakers, although relatively few in number, were a politically powerful force and their opposition to slavery led to Pennsylvania establishing the first emancipation statute in the United States. By the end of the eighteenth century, around 10,000 African-Americans had gravitated to Philadelphia, which, for its democratic ways, became known as the 'Athens of America'. The basic freedom from discrimination and freedom to worship appealed to many in the Old World who were victimized or oppressed because of their religious beliefs. Many of them set off to start new lives in what became the Commonwealth of Pennsylvania.

One such immigrant was Christopher Saxman, a deeply religious man, who, in 1764, left his home in Wittenberg in Germany to seek out a new life in America. He and his family sailed for the New World from the port of Rotterdam. A miller by profession, he settled near Latrobe in what is now

Westmoreland County, where he established one of the first flour mills in the region on the banks of the Loyalhanna River. Farmers from as far away as Pittsburgh employed his services and the hard-working Saxman built a shack where he and his wife raised a family of three sons and six daughters.

He saved enough from his labors to enable him to buy a 400-acre tract of land from the state in the Latrobe region. It was a tough life for a farmer, he and his family battling against the elements, wild beasts and marauding Native Americans. From time to time, such attacks forced the Saxman family to retreat to the fort at Latrobe. In spite of the depredations, Christopher Saxman persevered in cultivating his land, eventually establishing a homestead that would remain in his family for generations.

His eldest son, Mathias Saxman, who was born around 1770, took up his father's mantle, developing the property into a flourishing and self-sufficient farm with good deer hunting and fields of flax which the women of the household would spin into linen for summer wear. Winter clothing was of wool from their own sheep, the yarn again homespun and the garments home made.

Mathias and his wife Magdalena had ten children, the first of whom, Christopher, died in childhood, while another, Daniel, fell to his death from a hickory tree. As a result of these family tragedies, it was the couple's second son, Peter, born in 1803, who took over the family farm. An active member of the German Reform Church and a Democrat, he continued in the farming tradition until his death in 1871. It was one of Peter's sons, named Mathias after his grandfather, who would expand the family's holdings beyond their traditional homestead. While he worked the farm just as his father and grandfather had done, he spent every spare moment extracting as much of the coal on his land as he could. In those days, it was not unusual for farmers to scrape coal from their land. Because of the configuration of the hills in the rolling countryside, outcrops of coal were easy to find. Indeed, this rudimentary form of strip mining was even simpler than tunneling into a hillside or riverbank.

Until the middle of the nineteenth century, signs could often be seen on fence posts near farmers' primitive mines offering the opportunity to 'Dig Your Own Coal' for a price of 5 cents a bushel* or $1.25 a ton. It was an early equivalent of picking your own strawberries – and just as simple.

What set Mathias Saxman apart from his fellow farmers, however, was that he rolled up his sleeves and dug coal from the ground at a rate of around 250 bushels per day. He would load his haul on a wagon and transport it to the railroad station at Latrobe, where he shoveled it out to sell on in bulk. Within a short time he was employing men to help him mine the coal, and by the mid-1870s coal had taken over as the Saxmans' principal business. He formed a company with two partners, calling themselves M. Saxman & Company, and began to expand his business even further.

The shrewd businessman had seen the opportunities presented by the introduction of the Bessemer process, used to make steel, which was then replacing iron as industry's material of choice because of its strength and durability. This process, using an oxygen furnace, required coke – coal from which the gas has been extracted by a process of heating it – which burnt at much higher temperatures than coal. In 1880, just as American industry was booming, Saxman began building coke ovens. Within ten years, he had almost eighty in full production, thereby becoming one of the leading coal producers in Pennsylvania. He owned, controlled or developed the Saxman Coal and Coke Company, the Derry Coal and Coke Company, and the Superior Coal and Coke Company. In 1905 all of these companies were merged into the Latrobe-Connellsville Coal and Coke Company.

* In the US, a bushel is a unit of dry measure equivalent to 64 US pints or 0.03524 cubic meters (the Imperial bushel is slightly larger).

A sign of the family's wealth came in that same year when Saxman's son, Marcus, who had now joined the family business, bought, for $200,000, around 4,000 acres of land south-west of Indiana, known as the Jacksonville Field, from a local merchant named H. B. McIntire. His company built or took control of numerous mining towns, including the notorious Whiskey Run, which had a well-deserved reputation for lawlessness – by the mid-1920s, it was the site of approximately two dozen unsolved murders.

The younger Saxman himself was out to make a killing of a different kind. In the early years of the twentieth century, Marcus was not only involved in his father's extensive mining operations, but was also manager and treasurer of several other coal companies, as well as President of the Citizens' National Bank in Latrobe and Director of the Latrobe Trust Company.

In 1925, Marcus Saxman acquired a mine in Somerset County from the Quemahoning Creek Coal Company, owned by Charles Harrison and John Brydon, who had established a company town at the site twelve years earlier. Originally called Harrison, the town's name was later changed to Quecreek in order to avoid confusion with another town of the same name further north.

The mine at Quecreek was operated as the Saxman Number 2 mine and, by 1928, it employed 275 workers, producing around 500,000 tons of coal a year. By 1950, the number of employees had slipped to 250 and the mine's output was down to less than 200,000 tons per year. A world depression in the price of coal and fierce competition from other energy sources, principally oil, meant that by 1963 the mine was simply uneconomic. It closed that year, making around twenty-five miners jobless. Although it is not clear whether, by that time, the Saxmans were still mining the coal or merely owned the land, it signaled the end of an era for the family. Over the years, with falling prices and a general depression in the coal industry, they had moved away from coal mining. The Saxman Number 2 mine at Quecreek was the last mine they owned.

It had never been a happy place. Miners knew it as a wet mine, uncomfortable and cold to work in. As soon as the last remaining miners moved out, the water, that had plagued them when it was working, now began to gather in the old mine's dark and empty tunnels and chambers. This deadly accumulation of millions upon millions of gallons of stagnant ground water was to continue for almost forty years.

When Joseph Zambanini heard that they were opening up a new mine next door to the disused Saxman mine, he was filled with foreboding. He had worked at the mine in its heyday during the 1940s and remembered that water was a constant problem. Shortly before the mine closed, he had heard rumors that a belt of coal the size of a baseball diamond had been scooped out from an arca beyond the federal boundary line. Since the operation was illegal, it was not mapped. 'If they ever hit the old mine then they are going to be in big trouble,' the eighty-six-year-old retired miner warned.

Chapter III

NINE MEN DOWN

SINCE THE DAY he started work in the mines, Ron Schad has followed one golden rule – when the phone rings underground, answer it. 'A lot of guys will wait and see if somebody else is going to answer so that they don't have to crawl down to it,' he says. 'But it is one thing I believe in. It's your only contact with the outside world. It could be your wife was in a car wreck or your kids got hurt.' At around 8.30* on the evening of Wednesday, 24 July, Ron had just grabbed a ham salad sandwich from his lunch pail and was taking a brief break from loading coal on to the electric-powered shuttle car. That night's shift in the Mains section of Quecreek mine was going a whole lot better now that they had moved cuts.

Amid the din of the belt feeder and the noise of the continuous miner pounding away at the face, Schad could just hear the ringing of the phone fixed to the rib some twenty yards away. Then the loudspeaker attached to the silver instrument came alive as a voice called urgently; 'Mains, Mains, Mains – anybody? – Mains.' He put away his sandwich and drove the

*Inevitably, people's memories of the actual time of the initial inundation vary. Ron Hileman, for example, has said that the breach took place at 9.30, which in fact is *after* the alarm was raised. Where possible, I have relied on official logs, notably that kept by MSHA.

feeder car to a point near the phone, then he crawled on his hands and knees the rest of the way. In those long two minutes the amplified voice kept repeating; 'Mains, Mains – anybody there? – Mains.'

Reaching for the phone, he pressed the button to show that he could hear. There were no introductions, just a voice screaming, 'Get the fuck out! Get the fuck out! We hit water and it's coming. Get out and don't wait! I'm not kidding ya.' Ron Schad knew instantly that the voice belonged to Dennis 'Harpo' Hall, who was with the crew up at First Left, more than 500 feet above them and 2,000 feet to the south. Ron inwardly thanked God that Harpo had a voice like a foghorn and that he himself had earlier replaced the battery in the phone after it had been reported faulty. For Schad and the four-to-twelve crew, however, as for their coworkers, the nightmare was only just beginning.

Yet although he heard the terror and panic in Harpo's voice, he had no knowledge then of the magnitude of the disaster – or any appreciation of the courage that the other man had shown in spending a few precious minutes trying to warn his buddies rather than flee the raging water flooding First Left. 'I just had to do it,' Hall told him later. 'I knew you were gone if I didn't.'

In the space of a few moments the First Left mine section had been transformed into a Niagara of rushing water after Mo Popernack, the miner operator, had cut through the rock into the disused Saxman Number 2 mine. In doing so, he unleashed an underground reservoir containing an estimated 60 million gallons of stagnant water that threatened to sweep him and his crew away.

With blinding speed, thousands of gallons of stale yellowish liquid, barely recognizable as water, had burst over the top of his 5-ton machine, brushing it aside with malevolent force, turning his 20-foot wide section, known as Entry Number 6, into a furious, swirling torrent that rose rapidly as the section filled. Popernack, operating the continuous miner by remote control, was tucked behind a coal pillar when the first torrent exploded into the mine, and so was saved from being washed away. With the bright lights of the miner extinguished, he only had the flickering beam of his cap lamp to light the scene. What he saw frightened the life out of him, the torrent surging ominously towards the low mine roof, only 4 feet high at that point. He was immediately cut off from his coworkers, the terrifying surge of water racing past and over him, soaking him to the skin, and filling other entries and crosscuts, its force too much for one man to fight against without being swept away. Spotting Dennis Hall a few yards away in a loaded shuttle car, he yelled at him, 'Harpo, get out! Get the hell out of here now!'

Hall heard his friend's screams and drove the shuttle car away, making around 200 feet through the flood before the power died as the batteries short-circuited. In the seconds that passed following his shouted warning Popernack found that the force was too strong for him to follow without being swept to certain death. In the roaring darkness, his shouts were carried away in the fury of the cataract, so he used his cap lamp to signal to the others, moving his head from side to side to show that he couldn't follow them. He was stranded and isolated, crouching in the fierce current, swallowing mouthfuls of rancid air and knowing with a growing and ominous certainty that he was facing a wretched death.

Moments after the breach, the other miners, who were working at different crosscuts in the section, saw a wall of water hurtling towards them. 'When the water first broke through, I've never seen anything with so much rage in my entire life,' recalls John Unger. He and Ron Hileman, were perhaps 100 feet away, bolting the roof. Their earplugs and the noise of their drills had covered up the sound of the initial inundation. Then they saw the flood by the light of their cap lamps. 'A wall of water went past us, like a raging river,' Hileman later recalled.

Meanwhile, Tom 'Tucker' Foy was yelling warnings to the rest of the crew – 'Everybody out, we got water! We hit an old mine!' – his face livid with the effort. Crouching, all eight ran crab-like to the feeder at Entry Number 4, where the coal is dumped on to the conveyor belt that takes it outside. It is also the place where they are trained to gather in the event of an emergency.

'Call outside, call the other section,' crew boss Randy Fogle shouted at Hall who, having escaped the first rush of water, was nearest the phone. They knew that the other crew were working at a much lower level. While their own plight was desperate, if the other crew weren't warned they were dead men. Despite his own fears, Harpo made the call. In doing so, he saved the lives of the men working in the Mains.

In First Left, everyone was scared although no one was panicking . . . yet. They knew that their only hope of survival was to try to outrun the torrent that roared from the gash in the face. The most serious problem was that the exit shafts sloped down into a long curving dip before the ground gradually rose to the mouth of the mine. They faced a life-or-death race for survival, to beat the tide of water to the other side of the dip before it filled. If they could do that, they had a chance.

Crouching low, they plunged with racing hearts through the freezing water that was soon up to and then past their knees, its surging power threatening to pull them down with every step. They grabbed on to the conveyor belt and each other to keep from slipping into the torrent. Everyone was breathing hard, and the older men, John Unger and Tom Foy particularly, were beginning to feel severe pains in their chests. At one point Unger thought that he was going to have a heart attack. How much more, how much longer? they wondered, yet still the water continued to rise with a kind of remorseless malevolence.

'It was so noisy we couldn't hear each other scream,' Unger said later, with a shiver of remembrance. The eight men lurched and scrambled on to the now stilled conveyor belt, scrabbling and crawling over the coal, drenched with sweat as well as water, panting and praying. As Dennis Hall clambered on to the belt, the current nearly snatched his feet away. Randy Fogle, who was behind him, grabbed him by his raincoat and hauled him up.

They clawed their way along for somewhere between 2,000 and 3,000 feet, their hands cut and scratched from the loose coal on the belt before they realized that it was no use. 'We were trying to beat the water but it was traveling too fast,' Ron Hileman remembered. 'There was no way we were going to out-run it. It was at our feet, then up to our ankles, then getting higher. We were definitely scared.'

It was now that Blaine Mayhugh and John Phillippi, the two younger men leading the way, saw that the water had won. The deadly race was over. By the light of their cap lamps they could see that, a few yards ahead, it had reached the roof of the dip. Worse still, it was now backing up rapidly towards them. The two men signaled for the others to turn back. 'This isn't good, Blaine,' Tom Foy said to his son-in-law at one point. Mayhugh looked at him and replied, 'Yeah, I'm too young to die. I wanna see my wife and kids.' Exhausted and close to panic, the men now clawed their way back up the beltway, now fighting not only the driving current but the slope as well. Clinging to the belt to stop being swept away, gulping down a mixture of water spray and dank air, every yard was agony. At times the water reached to their necks, splashing around their mouths and noses, and they would find themselves swimming for a few yards in heavy sodden gear against a murderous riptide. 'Everybody was having a tough time because we about killed ourselves trying to get down there as fast as we could,' Randy Fogle remembers. At other places on the slope they craned their necks backwards to suck air from the roof crevices, water swirling around their ears and chins. Some used their hammers to give them purchase on the machinery; others, like John Unger, shed their equipment to give them more speed, or had it snatched from their bodies by the sheer weight of water. 'It was a terrible feeling,' Hileman recalled. 'That's when you start hoping and praying and getting scared.'

Now back in First Left, they split into groups, searching fruitlessly down different crosscuts for drier ground. Still the water kept rising. For a time in that first terrifying hour they tried to break through a solid wall built of 4-inch block in an attempt to gain entrance into another passageway, hoping to break out like that. By now Bob Pugh was the only one left with a hammer, and so he started pounding away. Then Fogle took a turn, and then, as he tired, Mayhugh and Phillippi. As the water rose Pugh was reduced to using his hammer under water in a desperate but hopeless attempt to smash a way through.

With the water still rising, they struggled on again, but no matter which way they went they seemed to be trapped. At one point they considered trying to break into the old Saxman mine – since it was at a higher elevation than the highest point of Quecreek, and since the water was rushing out of it, they felt that getting into the abandoned mine might afford them a chance to escape the worst of the flood. The plan was stillborn, however. The pitiless torrent, which had sapped their strength and their will, entirely filled the gash in the rock.

After what seemed like an eternity, but was in fact perhaps no more than an hour since the breach, they found temporary respite on higher ground deep inside the mine. All were soaked through, breathing hard and scared to death. Pugh and Unger had not stopped praying to themselves throughout their ordeal. Little Tucker Foy, his damaged heart pounding with effort, was exhausted, worn out with the exertion of simply trying to stay alive. They had waded, crouched, crawled and swum through a maze of low tunnels in a desperate search for escape. Yet there seemed to be no way out. As they paused to gather their thoughts and their breath, Tucker told them, 'If we have to run again, you guys go without me. I can't go.' His request was dismissed out of hand. They were all in this together. They would live or die as one. Their thoughts returned to the crew member they had left behind.

The urgency and raw fear in Dennis Hall's voice as he screamed down the phone to Ron Schad, working hundreds of feet below, was palpable. This was no false alarm or stupid prank. Like the crew in First Left, the men in the Mains were spread out, working on different tasks. Crouching, Schad stumbled over to Wendell Horner, his fellow shuttle-car operator, and yelled, 'Get the bolters, get the bolters! They hit water and we have to get out of here. Now!' While Wendell went to warn Doug Custer and Dave Petree, Schad, hunched over, ran as fast as he could in the confined space to where Joe Kostyk and Ryan Petree were working the continuous miner. He attracted their attention in the time-honored way by waving his cap lamp at them. Normally a miner would never shine a light at a fellow worker's face, as that would temporarily blind him. They always point the beam away from their eyes. Ryan heard him first. 'Shut it [the miner] off!' he roared at Kostyk. 'We got water. Get on the mantrip. Let's go.' Normally, Ron Schad is a man who likes to fool around, joking with the rest of the crew. This time they knew by the tone of his voice that he meant business.

Up ahead, Joe Kostyk was moving the cable that fed power to the continuous miner, ready to start a new cut in Entry Number 5. 'I heard someone screaming and yelling,' he recalls. 'Usually in coal mining when that starts somebody got hurt. I thought: "Oh man, what is going on?" Then I heard Ryan screaming "Get out of here! We got to get out of here now! They said they hit a bunch of water and it's coming our way."'

Kostyk responded at once, realizing instinctively that they were in deadly trouble. Still holding the remote control that maneuvers the miner, he crouch-ran for the battery-powered mantrip which, five hours earlier, had brought them into the mine. Ron Schad had already gone on to warn mechanic Larry Summerville, who was setting up the conveyor belt in another section. He had told Ryan not to bother switching off the power to the section or sorting out the canvas, the sheet used as part of the ventilation system to bring fresh air to the face. 'We can do that later,' he shouted, convinced that every second counted. If they found themselves in trouble with the mine bosses for not shutting down the section properly, he thought, then so be it.

Ryan, Joe, Dave, Wendell and Doug clambered aboard the mantrip and, with Ryan driving, headed up the common entry tunnel, the main highway from their section, Joe now cursing the fact that they had the slowest vehicle. Larry and Ron were slightly ahead on smaller golf cart-type vehicle, laboring up the sloping, 500-foot-long tunnel from the Mains section to the fork where it met the main exit shaft from First Left. They knew that Frank Stewart, their acting boss, was somewhere in the mine, although they hadn't seen him for a while. They also had to warn Barry Carlson, who was working a scoop some way back from the coalface. They hoped they could spot him on the way out. Ron saw him first, his scoop blocking their escape route, and shouted, 'Get the damn scoop out of the way! We got to get out of here.' At first Carlson didn't realize what was going on, and indicated that he wanted to drive out with the scoop. Schad shouted at him to leave it and join the others on the mantrip, which was now about 12 yards behind the golf cart. Carlson reversed his scoop into a crosscut and joined the five miners on the mantrip. 'I was scared,' Carlson admitted later. 'At the time I thought somebody got hurt in the section. I didn't know about water.'

In the blaze of the mantrip's headlamps they could make out Ron Schad and Barry Summerville ahead of them in the faster two-man golf cart. They had also spotted Frank Stewart in the distance, heading out of the mine on another golf cart. As Schad and Summerville reached the intersection of the travel-ways from the Mains and First Left, effectively the meeting of two major highways, they were greeted by a swollen river of water pouring down the slope from First Left. Like their work-mates in that section, they realized that their only chance of escape was to get past the lowest point of the slope before the torrent beat them to it.

They were too late. Ahead, they could see that the main travel-way was filled to the roof with water. They drove over to the belt-way which takes the coal to the surface. It was the same story. The belt was silent, its power shorted out by the water, and their cap lamps showed that the tunnel was full of water. Ron Schad remarked to Summerville, 'We're in deep shit now. We have to get out of here.' They realized that their only hope was to find the intake door that led to the ventilation shaft, a 3-foot-high tunnel running back towards the entrance, parallel to the belt-way and travelway, that brings fresh air into the mine. It is con-structed from cement-block walls built between the pillars to roof height, effectively forming two parallel walls, about 20 feet apart, which seal the shaft from the rest of the mine. If the shaft was dry, they still had a fighting chance of escape.

Summerville hurriedly backed up their vehicle for about 50 feet until they drew level with the intake door. Pulling it open they discovered that the air shaft was dry . . . for the moment. The others were still some way behind them, perhaps two min-utes. They parked the golf cart with its lights on facing the intake door, which they left open to indicate that that was their escape route. Then they entered the air shaft, knowing that if the block walls or the doors didn't hold, they were done for. As they started down the dip they could hear the water pouring down on either side along the 4-inch-thick walls. 'It sounded like thunder,' Ron recalled. Ominously, the pressure of the flood was forcing jets of water through every little gap in the block walls, threatening to overwhelm them. They knew that if a mandoor (a small door into a shaft, about 2 foot by 3 foot, which allows men to transfer from one section to another) or an intake door burst ahead of them, they would be engulfed by a tidal wave of water. With Ron leading, the two miners crawled as quickly as they could through the rising water. 'C'mon, c'mon, stop pissing around,' Ron yelled back at his friend, sounding close to panic.

Meanwhile, back on the mantrip, the other six miners still had no real sense of how precarious their position was. As soon as they reached the intersection with the First Left travelway, however, they were left in no doubt. 'The water was roaring,' Barry Carlson would remember. 'It was unbelievable.' At first Ryan tried to drive through it, but Barry yelled at him that they weren't going to make it. He stopped moving forwards and Joe Kostyk leapt off to check the condition of the beltway, splashing through the flood. As he recalled, 'I'll never forget the noise of that water coming down. My heart stopped when I saw it.' Like Summerville and Schad before them, they quickly realized that the main highways out of the mine were now under water. It was Dave Petree who screamed above the din, 'Get to the intake! We've got to get to the intake!'

They were now several hundred feet behind Larry and Ron, and in those few minutes the water inside the ventilation shaft had risen alarmingly. With the beltway and travelway blocked, they had no choice but to crawl through into the 3-foot-high intake tunnel, water pouring over the sill, spray hissing through the gaps between the blocks, the sound of a furious, pounding torrent beyond. It was terrifying. 'I knew we were in trouble,' Joe Kostyk admitted. 'It looked like we were trapped.' Worse still, they had to crawl down the dip into deeper water before they had any chance of escaping from the mine. The prospect was terrifying and, as Doug Custer remembered, 'As a crew we all hesitated.' They had crawled the distance of five crosscuts, maybe 150 to 200 feet, when ahead of them a man-door suddenly crashed open with a loud 'Boom!', water spewing from it like a fire hydrant on full force. Kostyk and Custer, who were leading the mantrip crew, paused, reluctant to traverse a section where the current was running so strongly. They knew, however, that they had to take their chance or die. There was no other choice, for now the shaft was filling with water.

Custer shouted, 'Let's go!' and he and Kostyk plunged into the icy current. It was much more powerful than either man had anticipated, and both were sucked into the swirling maelstrom. Doug lost his glasses, helmet and cap lamp and was bounced along the shaft floor by the current, badly bruising his hip. In between snatched breaths Joe Kostyk screamed at him, 'Get up and go, get up and go! Buddy, you're either going to swim or you're dying.' As Kostyk half-swam, half-crawled across the black torrent roaring out of the mandoor he thought about his wife and children and said to himself, 'I'm not dying in this coalmine. I'm not drowning, I'm not drowning in a coal mine. We're getting out of here.'

Numb, sodden and exhausted, they reached the other side of the river and waited for the others. In a matter of moments Dave and Ryan Petree, Wendell Horner and Barry Carlson plunged after them. 'Just come through it, fellas, come through it – you got to get through it,' Kostyk shouted in encouragement. Their lights flickered to and fro as the miners grabbed cables, pipes, bolt heads, anything to give them purchase. Suddenly Barry Carlson's light went out, the fifty-seven-year-old miner sucked under the water by the force of the current which tossed him around 'like a gumball'. For a few terrifying moments he thought that he too, like his brother Robert years earlier, would end up dying in the mines. The sheer power of the current kept him from getting his head out of the water, and the weight of his waterlogged clothing held him under. Fortunately Dave Petree had seen his friend go under and crawled back for him. With one hand holding a nearby cable to stop himself from being washed away, he used his free hand – he had attached his self-rescuer to his belt rather than carry it – to yank Barry out of the water, grabbing him by the waist. They crouched there motionless for a few moments, Dave using all the strength in his upper body to hold on to the cable with his other hand, against the dead weight of his friend and the pull of the current. Then his son Ryan joined in the rescue, pulling Barry by the arm so that between the two of them they were able to manhandle him across the worst of the flood in a ragged human chain. 'If I hadn't been helped I would have been in big trouble,' says Barry, with dry understatement.

Although the bursting of the mandoor had threatened to drown them, what they did not realize at the time was that it had relieved the pressure on the block walls. If it hadn't blown open, the adjoining walls would probably have collapsed – with catastrophic consequences. The only hope they had was for the walls to hold. Even when they had crossed that first torrent they knew they weren't safe, with the water thundering past the walls outside and jetting through the gaps. 'You just knew there was a force behind those walls that you didn't want anything to do with,' Joe Kostyk said later. 'We saw its teeth. We knew it was there to hurt you, to kill us. To a man we knew that if one of those walls had blown out we were going to die.'

A few feet ahead the mine dipped – 'a roll in the coal' – before the slope at last continued upwards. If they could crawl that distance they had a chance of making it out alive. Kostyk remembered praying: 'I just kept thinking to myself, "Just give us a few more steps, God, just give us a few more steps and we'll make it."' With the floor of the shaft now inches deep in water, they crawled and scuttled as fast as they could, every muscle aching, their chests pounding, their mine clothes sodden and heavy. Suddenly they heard the frightening 'Boom!' sound again as another mandoor blew open somewhere behind them.

Now, with every step, they knew that they might be engulfed by a wall of water.

Nerves jangling, they made it through the dip and continued onwards up the slope. After about 300 feet or so they found themselves outside a third mandoor, which led to a travelway where the roof was higher. At that time they had no way of knowing how long the intake walls would hold, nor did they know what would greet them on the other side of the door. Hesitantly, Joe Kostyk approached the mandoor, listening hard for the sound of water on the other side. Then, as he had been taught in safety training, he carefully put his hand on the metal, feeling for any tell-tale vibrations. Finally, he gingerly opened the door into the travelway, which was close to Entry Number 5. His cap lamp revealed that the passage was dry, then, at almost the same moment, he spotted ahead of him the lights of Larry Summerville and fire boss Frank Stewart, waiting anxiously for them. 'I've never been happier to see two guys in my whole life,' Kostyk would say later. 'We all came up through that door and we were all scared.' They huddled together and checked that everyone was all right. A few moments earlier Larry and Frank had used the phone at the head of the beltway to call for help and to try to raise the crew in First Left. They had heard the ominous sound of the mandoors bursting open below, and feared the worst. As they did a quick head count they realized that one man was missing – Ron Schad.

The former Marine had been crawling ahead of Larry Summerville, who was himself a few hundred feet ahead of the men from the mantrip. Every so often he had shouted at Larry to hurry up, waving his cap lamp in a circular motion to indicate that it was safe to follow. He and Summerville had crawled past the first mandoor just before it had blown open. Schad had looked back then and, though he could see nothing, he had heard the sound of gushing water 'like Niagara Falls and thunder'. He pressed on with greater urgency, scared, but also

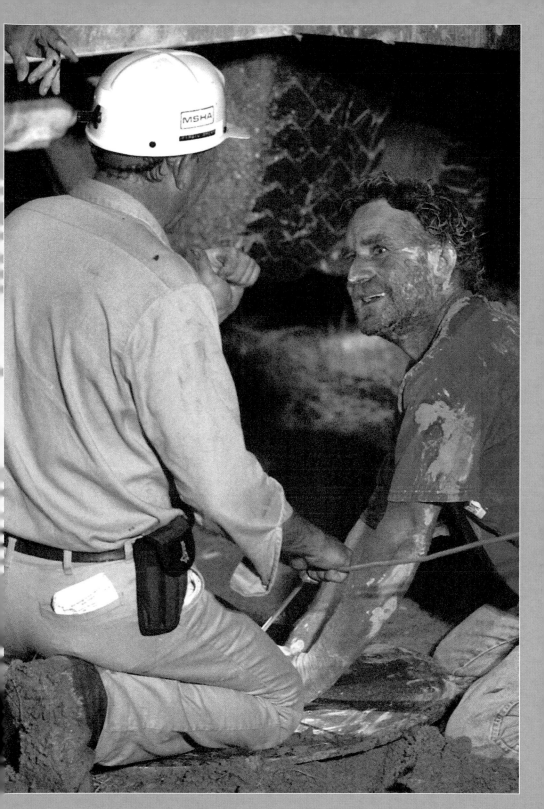

Jubilation when, on 27 July, rescue workers first hear voices after lowering a microphone to the nine miners trapped 240 feet below ground, after flooding in the mine where they were working

Main photo: Bill and Lori Arnold's farm, where the rescue shafts were drilled down to the trapped miners

The nine men whose ordeal captured the world's attention. *Anti-clockwise from top left*: Mark Popernack; Dennis Hall; Robert Pugh with his girlfriend, Cindy Thomas; Randy Fogle (*left*) and John Unger; Ron Hileman; Blaine Mayhugh; Thomas Foy; John Phillippi

Main photo: Quecreek, Pennsylvania – small-town America that became the focus of world attention

Six of the nine miners who escaped the inundation. *Anti-clockwise from top left*: Ryan Petree; his father, Dave Petree; Joe Kostyk (*left*) and Ron Schad; Ron Schad, who still suffers nightmares about his lucky escape, back in the mine gallery from which he crawled during the flooding; Doug Custer; Barry Carlson

Top: Joe Sbaffoni, a key figure in the rescue, with Governor Mark Schweiker

Center: The flooded portals of Quecreek No. 1 mine

Bottom: Planning the rescue: Governor Schweiker and senior members of the team consult the maps of Quecreek No. 1. *Left to right*: the Governor; David Lauriski, MSHA; Richard Stickler, Director of Pennsylvania's Bureau of Deep Mine Safety; Ray McKinney, MSHA

Right, top: Rescue worker Tony Gibbons pounds on a pipe with a hammer in an attempt to make contact with the trapped miners

Center: Some of the members of the Mine Safety and Health Administration who took part in the rescue. First row: Amy Louviere with John Urosek on her right; behind: Gerry Davis (*in gray suit*) with Joe Tortorea on his right

Bottom, left: Drill workers adjust the rig as the 30-inch-wide hole is drilled

Bottom, right: The 30-inch drill bit being lowered into position — a day later it broke

Tension and tiredness show on rescue workers' faces as time begins to run out

desperate to get help for his friends. All the while the water heaved and surged against the intake walls. When he heard the 'Boom!' of the second door bursting he feared that the rest of his crew had drowned and that in a few moments he too would be swallowed up in the swirling, filthy flood. 'This is when I asked God to grab a hold of me and help me out,' he confessed, his voice breaking at the memory of the horror that he and his fellow miners endured. '"Get me out," I prayed.'

Fearing what lay behind the third mandoor, which the others, including Summerville behind him, later used as an escape hatch, Schad stayed inside the intake shaft and crawled on his hands and knees for a mile, several times smashing his head on the roof, which at some places was as low as 32 inches. At some point he threw off his heavy rubberized raincoat, reasoning that if the water caught him he would not need it; indeed, it might hamper his movements or even pull him under. At last his cap lamp lit up the green reflectors set at regular intervals along the walls to guide miners outside in case of smoke or fire. 'I was terrified,' he admitted. 'I had chest pains, I knew I should stop and rest, but I thought that I would rather die of a heart attack than drown, because when you drown you have a couple of seconds to think about it and fight it.'

Schad began to follow the reflectors until, after an age – perhaps forty minutes since he had entered the shaft, or a little longer – bleeding from hands, elbows, knees and head, exhausted and in shock, he made it to the mouth of the mine, where he too used a phone to raise the alarm, calling the supervisor in the mine office. He was still on his own, still anxious about the fate of his friends. It would be a few minutes before the rest of the crew joined him.

When they had regrouped by Entry Number 5, the eight other miners knew that they were still in danger. Not only were they being pursued by the rising water, but they also recognized that they might be overcome by poisonous fumes pushed ahead by the deluge. While methane gas is rightly feared as the cause of many underground explosions, miners also have cause to fear 'black damp', air without oxygen, which can suffocate in seconds and arrives without warning. All eight clambered on to Frank Stewart's two-man golf cart and sluggishly made their way to the mouth of the mine, where an exhausted Ron Schad was waiting for them. He flung his arms around Joe Kostyk and told him, 'When I heard that door go I thought you guys were dead. Gone.'

Even as they were relieved to be reunited with no one missing, they were perplexed that the nine men of the other crew had failed to muster outside the mine. After all, they had been working at a much higher level than the four-o'clock shift, and closer to the pit entrance. Once they had caught their breath they went to the several mine entrances, known as 'portals', looking for the tell-tale light from cap lamps that would signal that the crew from First Left had made it. None showed. It was a puzzle; worse, it was deeply worrying.

Back at the mine entrance, the alarm had been raised, and calls for assistance had already gone out. The Mains crew considered their next move. Although they were traumatized, soaked and chilled to the bone, their first instinct was to go back into the mine to try to rescue their buddies. It was a reaction typical of miners in general, and of the Quecreek crews in particular.

One of them suggested heading back down in a mantrip. That was immediately ruled out. They knew that the flood was rising fast – indeed, they had only just escaped with their lives – and they feared that the water would push deadly methane and other inflammable gases ahead of it. It would only take a spark from a battery-powered vehicle like a mantrip and they wouldn't just have a flood. They would have an explosion and a fire, which would kill them and the nine missing miners, who they still believed were heading out of the mine.

While several of the crew sat in silence, stunned and exhausted, others ventured cautiously on foot some way back down the various exit and entrance shafts of the mine. Their shouts brought no welcome response, the light from their cap lamps picked out no signs of life. As they searched, alarms deeper inside the mine began shrieking as oxygen monitors were triggered either by bad air or by the encroaching flood tide, which shorted out the electric cables. It made an eerie and chilling accompaniment to their futile search.

Outside in the darkness, someone muttered a prayer.

Chapter IV

BOYS IN THE BUBBLE

WITH HIS SHOCK OF swept-back silver-gray hair and twinkling blue eyes, Gerry Davis looks like everyone's favorite uncle. Among colleagues at his office in Hunker, Pennsylvania, the jaunty sixty-year-old has a reputation for light-hearted teasing. Yet the ready smiles, the banter and joshing, do not tell the whole story, for Davis has witnessed more than his fair share of tragedy and heartache. A miner for seven years, he has worked for the federal Mine Safety and Health Administration, a division of the US Department of Labor, for most of his career. It was the Sunshine mine disaster in Idaho in 1972, which claimed ninety-one lives, that helped bring about sweeping reforms in underground mining, including, ultimately, the creation of MSHA. As an assistant district manager for MSHA Number 2 district, which includes Somerset County, Davis is in the front line whenever there is a mine accident, explosion, fire – or inundation.

Years of salutary experience have taught him that all too often mine rescues end only in the recovery. In his fifteen years with MSHA, thirty-nine bodies have been brought out at incidents he has attended. The pattern is almost always the same; the initial budding of hope slowly giving way before the almost insuperable difficulties of underground rescue, and finally yielding to the unrelenting reality of death, sorrow and despair.

At 9.40 on the evening of Wednesday, 24 July, Gerry was at home pondering the lessons in his Bible, for he reserves the half-hour before he retires for the night at 10 as his time for devotional studies. While he cannot recall the passage he was reading at the time, he does remember his reaction when MSHA staff assistant Carol Boring called. He knew instantly that something was wrong by the urgent tone in her voice. 'We have an inundation at Quecreek mine. There are nine miners down,' she told him. 'I'm on my way,' he replied, shaking his head in quiet disbelief at the news. Once again Somerset County, only 1,000 square miles in total and with a population of just 80,000, was going to make the headlines for all the wrong reasons. Less than a year earlier, the United Airlines Flight 93 had crashed at Shanksville, not much over 10 miles from Quecreek, during the 9/11 hijackings, its passengers and crew giving their lives to thwart the terrorists. Now this. Nine men lost, nine frightened families wondering, hoping and waiting. 'I went from devotion to emotion. The adrenalin started pumping,' recalls Gerry, who inwardly said a prayer before he left the house, clutching a ham and cheese sandwich that his wife, Judy, had hastily made for him.

In the car on the way to the MSHA office in Hunker, his mind ran over the main factors affecting a rescue attempt; how the mine was laid out, the flow of water, the elevation, likely escape routes and, most important, where the men might be if they had managed to survive the initial flood.

The same vital questions were swirling round the head of fellow MSHA assistant district manager Kevin Stricklin as he raced the forty miles along the Pennsylvania Turnpike from Hunker towards the mine site. Known as 'the Duke' because of his John Wayne drawl and craggy good looks, Stricklin, forty-four, had spent much of the year investigating the cause of the devastating fire at the Jim Walters mine in Birmingham, Alabama, in September 2001, which killed thirteen miners. He hoped that this was not going to be a rerun of that tragedy. 'I got a knot in my stomach as soon as I heard the news,' recalled Stricklin, who at that time was in overall command of the rescue. 'I was hoping against hope that I would get a second call to say that it was a false alarm, the nine guys were safe. It never came.'

While Stricklin, Davis and another federal colleague, MSHA engineer John Urosek, headed for the mine, mine owner and superintendent Dave Rebuck was already making calls for help and pulling out maps in his cluttered office, which overlooks the mine site. He had been getting ready for bed when, at a little after nine o'clock, his wife Annette handed him the phone. The call was from the 'outby' guy (the mechanic on duty, so called because he works out by the machines) from the mine. They had trouble, he told Rebuck. Big trouble. The mine was flooding. Nine guys underground, possibly trapped. It was the beginning of four days of living hell for Rebuck. Those who know him well say that his graying, Kris Kristofferson-style beard and hair literally turned fully gray in that time.

From his car during the thirty-minute journey to his mine, he alerted federal and state officials to the emergency, setting in motion a full-scale rescue operation that would ultimately involve more than three hundred men and women. At 9.45 p.m., according to the MSHA log, he was met at the mine by mine supervisor Joe Hoffman, who lived a couple of miles away, and Lynn Jamison, district mine manager for the Pennsylvania Bureau of Deep Mine Safety. Hard on their heels was John Weir, land manager for PBS Coal, the parent company that had originally leased out the Quecreek mine to a business consortium which included Weir and Rebuck.

As they pored over the mine maps under the strip lighting in Rebuck's office, the telephone began to ring almost continuously. One of the first calls they received was from Jamison's immediate boss, Joe Sbaffoni, head of the Bituminous Division of the state's Deep Mine Safety Bureau. Over the next few days he was to become the very public, if initially reluctant, face of the rescue operation. At that point, however, he knew as much – or as little – about the disaster as everyone else.

'What have we got, Dave?' Sbaffoni asked, as he paced around the kitchen of his home in Fairchance in Fayette County, south of Pittsburgh. Rebuck tersely told him that eighteen miners had been caught underground after an inundation at the mine. Nine had escaped. Nine were trapped. And the water was rising fast. 'My heart went into my stomach,' Sbaffoni remembers. 'You feel pretty helpless when you get that kind of water coming. It's bad when you get explanations like that over the telephone.'

It was painfully apparent that the odds were stacked heavily against the men underground. The old Saxman mine they had breached was higher than the point at which they were had been working. This meant that even if they hadn't been swept away in the initial flood, they would probably drown as the water from the abandoned mine filled up the newer, and deeper, Quecreek workings. It was just a matter of time. For the moment their only possible chance of survival was if they had managed to find high ground within the Quecreek mine. Even so, that would only bring them breathing space – literally. In the course of Sbaffoni's hurried conversation with Rebuck it became clear that the rescuers' only hope was to locate the highest point of the Quecreek mine, and then drill down to it. That would give them a chance, albeit a very slim one. As soon as he put the phone down Sbaffoni drove to his office in Uniontown to consult with his superior, Richard Stickler, Director of the Bureau of Deep Mine Safety, and mining engineers Tom McKnight and Bill Bookshar. In the meantime, Weir called Jim Alumbaugh, a retired miner well known locally for his extensive collection of old mine maps, to see if he had any charts, deeds or other documents that might help in the search for the men, and which might also explain the reason for the inundation.

Hoffman and Jamison, the men on the ground at Quecreek Number 1, knew that the odds were stacked against them from the moment they saw the faces of the nine miners who had escaped. Aching, exhausted and shocked, they poured out their harrowing story as they trooped disconsolately into the lamp room. Dave Rebuck, conscious that news of the disaster was going to hit the media soon, told his men to call home.

It was 9.40, perhaps 80 minutes after the breach, when Diana Schad's phone rang. As soon as she picked up she knew that something was wrong. Her husband's voice was strained and distant. In clipped tones, Ron told her that they had trouble down the mine but that he and Joe Kostyk, his next-door neighbor, were fine, and asked her to go and tell Joe's wife Andrea that her husband was safe and unhurt. When she tried to question him he replied that he couldn't tie up the phone. Then told her he loved her, and hung up. One by one, the other miners called their loved ones to say that they were safe. Ron Schad recalled the atmosphere in the lamp room with weary clarity: 'Everybody was just so shaken up. Everybody was afraid, and the company guys were afraid for us. They thought we could have had heart attacks or go into shock. We just sat there a bit and prayed and cried.'

By now Dave Rebuck's concern that news of the flood was spreading, and would soon seep into the media, was being amply justified. Shortly after ten o'clock a rookie reporter, Leona Kozuch, who was about to leave the offices of the local *Daily American* newspaper in Somerset, was handed an e-mail by the newsdesk which said that nine miners had been injured at a mine near Quecreek. Since she lived near there she went to take a look. Apart from a state trooper guarding the private road leading to the mine all seemed quiet, but a call to her uncle, who worked at the mine, confirmed and expanded upon the story, which she filed to her paper. It made a few paragraphs on the *Daily American*'s front page the following day.

That original e-mail had been sent out by the Somerset County 911 communications center, which was now alerting all emergency services to the plight of the nine trapped men. At 9.53 an ambulance was dispatched to the mine from Somerset, while police and fire officers were also informed. At his home on a hillside above the Quecreek mine, Mark Zambanini, the Sipesville fire chief, was roused from his slumbers by a shrill bleep from his pager. The message asked him to call the communications center. 'I knew immediately that it was out of the ordinary, something that they didn't want to put out on the air,' he says. 'When they do that people with scanners listen in and everyone flocks to the incident.' It was way too late for such precautions, however. Shortly afterwards, as Zambanini was briefing his fellow fire officers at Sipesville, TV cameraman Mike Drewecki, who works for the NBC affiliate station WPXI out of Pittsburgh, was scrambling to Quecreek. This was to be the third mine disaster he had covered. The other two had ended in tragedy. Mentally, he prepared himself for long faces and a long night.

So too did Zambanini's wife Robin, head of Sipesville fire station's Ladies' Auxiliary Section, who learned that the state police had decided to use the century-old white clapboard fire hall as a gathering point for the families of the missing miners. Corporal Robert Barnes Jr of the state police was busily calling the nine families and asking them to assemble in Sipesville, blandly telling them that there had been an 'incident' at the mine, and that he had no other information. When Denise Foy got the news she immediately called her daughter, Leslie Mayhugh, who was on the point of taking a bath before her husband Blaine returned home from his shift. 'Leslie, there's been an accident at the mine,' her mother told her. 'Your dad is trapped underground.' Leslie was stunned. 'But, Mom, what are you talking about? Blaine is there as well.' Denise Foy's call marked the start of a waking nightmare for both women.

Leslie roused her children, Kelsey and Tyler, and together they waited for Blaine's parents, Blaine Sr and Margie, to pick them up. A hair-raising ride in the older Mayhugh's Ford Taurus brought them to the fire hall in record time, Leslie fretting all the while about what kind of trouble her husband and father faced.

For Sue Ellen Unger, who suffers from multiple sclerosis, learning and acting upon the news proved to be a rather more long-winded process. Her debilitating illness prevents her from moving around without the aid of a walker or, sometimes, a wheelchair. So by the time she managed to get to the shrilly ringing telephone that evening Corporal Barnes had simply left a terse and rather vague message for her to go to the fire hall in Sipesville. She slowly struggled into her car, thinking all the while that she was simply going there to pick up her husband and then bring him home. The reality was very different, however. When she entered the fire hall in Sipesville she saw two pastors, Barry Ritenour, who has two Methodist churches in Somerset County, and Joseph Beer, of Laurel Mountain United Church of Christ, who lived a couple of stone's throws away from the fire hall. She saw other volunteers, too, there to lend whatever help and comfort they could, practical or emotional. Their presence, together with the muted attendance of some of the other miners' families – among them Cathy Hileman, and Sandy Popernack with her two sons, Luke and Dan – brought home to Sue Ellen that there would be no easy homecoming. For John Weir, who was given the difficult job of briefing the families, the first time he walked into the fire hall was, he recalls, 'the worst moment of my life'. The news, admittedly very sketchy, was about as bleak as it could be. He told them about the flood and said that the rescue team was working on the theory that the men had moved to high ground inside the mine. Before he left he promised them that everyone was doing the very best they could to bring their loved ones home. A little while later, when Doug Custer, who had been asked to speak to the families, walked in, the reality of their loved ones' predicament began to sink in. Even though he tried to downplay the scale of the inundation, nobody was fooled. They could see by the cuts and bruises on his body and the numb shock in his eyes that he and his coworkers had been to hell and back. It did not take much imagination to visualize what their men were going through. One volunteer from the Ladies' Auxiliary Section, taking pity on Custer's obvious distress, put her arms around him and hugged him. Everyone in the fire hall began to fear the worst.

It was now around 11.30, and the scene that greeted Joe Hoffman when he left John Rebuck's office and went down to the mouth of the mine only confirmed that fear. He and other mine inspectors went through the elaborate but necessary safety checks, testing for oxygen levels, methane and other explosive, poisonous or suffocating gases, before they could allow anyone to proceed further into the mine. With the safety checks completed to their satisfaction, Hoffman and mechanic Larry Summerville, who had escaped only two hours earlier, went back into the mine from the highest entry point to assess the conditions at first hand. It was a mission that nearly ended in tragedy. Hoffman dropped Summerville off at a telephone point, asking him to keep trying to call First Left, while he ventured deeper into the mine on one of the two-man golf carts. Underestimating the speed at which the flood was rising, he went too far down and, as water came roaring in from another section, was forced to beat a hasty retreat. Shining his cap lamp at the approaching water, he glimpsed a miner's raincoat and a pair of rubber gloves floating on the current. For a moment he thought he was looking at a corpse. They proved to be only articles long abandoned in the mine, but it was an unnerving moment. The omens looked increasingly foreboding.

At around the time that Hoffman and Summerville were forced back by the onrushing water, and a mile or so further in the mine, Mark Popernack was considering his own dire options. Unable to join his eight companions as they tried to escape, he had been alone with only his thoughts – and his prayers – for the last three hours, waiting in the pitch darkness, listening helplessly as the water roared past him.

Conscious of the need to save the battery for his cap lamp, he switched it on only occasionally to scan the rushing waters, trying to see whether they had diminished at all. The sight that greeted him struck fear into his soul. Far from slackening, the torrent was rising inexorably towards him. If he didn't do something soon the water would claim him. Reasoning that it was better to die attempting to escape the flood than let the water simply overwhelm him, he hooked the water hose from the now wrecked continuous miner under his armpits to give him balance and stepped gingerly out into the savage current. Then he took another step. He knew in his heart that his third step would be his last. For a long moment he hesitated. Then, about 20 feet away on the other side of the torrent, he saw the welcome beam of a miner's cap lamp. The cavalry had arrived in the unlikely shape of John Unger, who began yelling at him to go back to his former position. 'That was one of my prayers that was answered,' Popernack remarked later.

The other eight, who had broken through a 4-inch-thick cinderblock wall to reach their buddy, had a plan in mind to save him, albeit a desperate one. They aimed to use the scoop, which is normally used to pick up coal and deliver supplies around the mine, to cross the flood, pick up Popernack and haul him back to their side. For the moment, however, in spite of Popernack's urgings, the waters were running too fast even to consider an attempt at rescue. Finally, Randy Fogle decided to give it a try. 'I don't know about this, Fogle,' said John Unger as the crew chief gently eased the unwieldy machine into the water. He had visions of both men and the machine being swept away by the current, he and the rest of the crew simply helpless spectators.

Popernack, the lightest of the crew, watched intently as the scoop, buffeted by the force of the water, gradually edged towards him. As it came within range he coiled himself and then leapt forwards, landing in the machine's upturned bucket. The scoop jolted with his weight but held fast in the current. Fogle carefully reversed out of the current to safety, guided by the lamps of the other miners. 'That was the first miracle of the night because I wanted everybody together,' recalled Fogle. Now they were nine again. Even so, once the hugs of reunion were over, the knowledge that they were in terrible danger flooded back.

Just how terrible was painfully obvious to the grim-faced men who had assembled for a midnight conference in Dave Rebuck's prefabricated office, which was, for the moment, the command center. Gathered round the maps on the table were Kevin Stricklin, Gerry Davis, John Urosek, Dave Rebuck, state mines inspector Ellsworth Pauley and engineer Jim Beisinger, both from the state's Deep Mine Safety Bureau. Stricklin, who was in overall command, was well aware of the heavy responsibility: 'It was on my plate and I felt the burden of the world on my shoulders. We were in a pretty bad predicament. Very bad. There was a very good chance that the miners would have been killed by the brute force of the water or swept away and drowned.'

All the known facts indicated that the odds were stacked against them. At that time they vaguely knew of only two other recent mine inundations: one in Germany, where miners had mistakenly drilled into the North Sea, and another in India, where the bottom of a lake had been breached. Both had ended in tragedy. The inundation at Quecreek looked to be heading the same way. An initial reading of the water level showed that it was at 1,810 feet above sea level, close to the mine's entrance, as Joe Hoffman had discovered. By their rough calculations

200,000 gallons of water – equivalent to the pumping power of 200 fire engines – was pouring into Quecreek mine every single minute. This stark data was thrown at Dr Kelvin Wu and his technical team who, in response to the emergency, had assembled at the MSHA office in Hunker, near New Stanton. Over the telephone, they were asked one question: How long have we got? Their answer confirmed everybody's worst fears. Hours. At the most. As John Urosek remembers, 'Our hearts were in our mouths. The water was rising, the clock was ticking and we needed to do something quickly.'

Yet their options were severely limited. There was some talk of using Navy divers, but since none were immediately available, and it would take hours to get them there with their equipment, that plan was quickly ruled out. Anyway, it was too risky – although the team would later come back to this idea. The rescue planners briefly discussed drilling into the old Saxman mine in case the trapped miners had sought refuge there, but a calculation of the force of the incoming water led them to abandon that plan as well. They kept coming back to one choice – to drill into the highest point of the Quecreek mine, around Entry Number 4, close to where the original inundation had occurred, in the hope that the trapped men had made it to there. It was, perhaps, a forlorn hope, but it was the one practical chance the rescuers had. 'We all pointed to the same place on the map,' recalls Stricklin, 'and I asked God for any help he could give us.'

Certainly fate was initially kind to them. The spot they had chosen as the optimum point at which to drill a 6-inch borehole was directly between a graveyard, a farm pond and a main road. Had it lain a few yards either side, they would have had insurmountable problems. What also worked in their favor was the fact that the mine maps were up to date and accurate, a tribute to the largely unsung work of mine surveyor Chad Mostoller, whose mapping was, as one rescuer noted, 'right on the money'.

In fact, he had surveyed the underground workings only two days before. They had another advantage in the shape of mine superintendent Dave Rebuck and engineer Joe Gallo, who not only knew every inch of the workings, but also knew the trapped men well, and were able to second-guess how Fogle and company might have reacted to the crisis. As an added advantage, Rebuck and Gallo had well-thumbed books of contacts, and in anticipation of the growing rescue operation had set to work calling the local drill companies, engineers and technicians who would locate the point on the surface that corresponded precisely to the position of the highest point of the mine.

By additional luck, Rebuck's friend Sean Isgan, once a champion wrestler but now the owner of CME Engineering, had yet to take his annual summer hiking trip. His company specializes in using global-positioning (GPS) equipment to locate positions on the earth's surface with great accuracy. It was to be his job that night to find the point on the surface that directly corresponded to the highest point inside the mine, which the men in the command center had agreed was the most likely place where Fogle and company would have headed. Isgan's expertise would be vital, his calculations perhaps meaning the difference between life and death – literally. Rebuck heaved a huge sigh of relief when he found Isgan still at his home in Somerset.

In the meantime the county's 911 communications center had joined in the search for drills, pumps and riggers. One dispatcher, Jeremy Coughenoun, remembered that his former Sunday-school teacher, Judy Bird, worked for Sperry Drilling. His call reached her at home at 10.45, and she immediately drove round to the home of her general manager, Rich Little. By midnight he, Bird and other Sperry employees were at the mine with a drill truck and casing. So too was Louis Bartels, who runs a small drilling company based in the nearby town of Somerset, and who had been called to the command center at about 10.45.

The old adage that everyone in Somerset County is related – or at least connected – to someone else in the county proved not only to be true, but to be vital as the rescue effort intensified.

Little Morgan Arnold was in the middle of a nightmare. Presumably the three-year-old was not dreaming about puddles. His cries woke his father, Bill Arnold, who stumbled from his bed at about 12.30 and went to his son. Once he had soothed the boy he got back into bed, quietly pleased that he could snag another three hours' sleep before he had to get up to start the milking. No sooner had he settled down to sleep, however, than Pitch, their mongrel dog, started barking. It sounded like a bark of alarm rather than a conversation with the other mutts in the neighborhood. Wearily Bill climbed from his bed and looked out the window from which, to his surprise and annoyance, he saw several vehicles parked by his boundary fence and men with torches wandering around on his land.

His first thoughts was that the intruders were up to no good. He dressed quickly, roused his wife Lori and told her to stay near the phone, and then woke his eldest daughter's boyfriend, Scott, who was sleeping on the couch downstairs. Grabbing his trusty Colt .45 from its hiding place, he and Scott swung into his pickup and headed off for what they thought was going to be an early-morning confrontation. Confrontation quickly changed to confusion when he realized that two of the apparent strangers were friends, Sean Isgan and his fellow surveyor Bob Long. Without preamble, they explained to the farmer that nine miners were trapped beneath his land and that they needed to drill urgently, indicating the rough location. 'What can I do to help?' Bill Arnold asked in reply, all thought of sleep banished. While Long unloaded some of the $60,000 worth of high-tech kit from the back of his Blazer, Arnold used a chainsaw to remove a fence and a 14-foot cherry tree that would be in the drillers' way.

Isgan and Long knew they had to stay absolutely focused. They also knew that they had to be right. Nine lives depended on their skills. A life-or-death game of 'find the needle in the haystack' was under way – and the clock was ticking. 'We were literally scared to death,' recalls Isgan. From the mine map, they had already been given the coordinates underground for the point where the rescue team believed the miners had gone to escape the flood. This was the highest point inside Quecreek Number 1. Now Isgan and Long had to find the corresponding point above ground. They had already established some coordinates in the next field in order to obtain a general fix on their position. Once all the coordinates had been entered into Long's laptop they could be translated into the GPS system. Satellites overhead would then beam down the information to a tripod-mounted transmitter, which in turn relayed the data to a hand-held device called a 'rover'.

Like some latter-day water diviner, Long, holding the rover, strode purposefully to the spot on the surface which, according to the miracles of modern science, was 231 feet directly above the point which, a couple of hours earlier, Kevin Stricklin had pointed to on the underground mine map. They checked, rechecked and then triple-checked their calculations. Finally, with enormous trepidation, Long drove a stake into the ground just three yards from the country road leading to the Arnold farm.

Although the chosen drill spot had missed the farm pond, the cemetery and the main road, Bill Arnold feared that it was directly above a main gas pipe that had been laid years before. Precious minutes were lost while a metal detector was found and Arnold hauled out an old digger – normally used to bury the occasional cow – and set to work digging a trench in order to locate the pipe. In the event, they failed to find it, which at least meant that it was not in the area where they wanted to drill.

As the minutes ticked by, the car park at the nearby Casebeer church was becoming a hive of activity as an assortment of fire engines, rescue trucks and media vans began to assemble there, the whole scene now lit by the unholy glow of emergency arc lights. More time was lost because electronic signals from cell phones and other equipment seemed to be interfering with the information Bob Long and Sean Isgan were sending to their own satellite. 'Some of the reporters initially were rude and interrupted what I had to do with the GPS system,' Long later complained. 'At first the media set up right at the site but the satellite trucks knocked out my radio.' In the early hours of the morning, however, state troopers moved the media to the disused Giant Eagle supermarket three miles down the road towards Somerset.

Finally, Isgan and Long agreed that the spot where they had hammered in a stake was where the five-strong Bartels crew should start drilling. Both men were racked with anxiety. 'What if we'd have been off by three feet and hit one of the mine pillars?' Long later said on CNN TV. 'We'd have had no idea it was a pillar, or if we'd missed the tunnel by an inch or a mile. Basically we'd have had to throw all the maps into the trash and drill ten feet this way, ten feet that way, until we found the tunnel. Who knows how long it might have taken?'

With the stake in place, Louis Bartels, who has twenty-nine years' experience in drilling, backed his rig on to the site and got to work. It was now 2.50 in the morning. There was not a moment to lose. Working by the light of the full moon and the lamps that had been rigged, driller Alex Nicoletti chewed into the earth, dedicating every ounce of power in the truck-mounted rig to driving the 6-inch bit through rock, soil and gravel. 'It was awesome to see,' said Bill Arnold, who had now opened up his whole farm to the rescue effort.

Equally frantic was the activity in the command center back at the mine as calls were made for the whole panoply of specialist equipment and personnel needed in any rescue attempt. From drills to pumps, seismic measuring equipment, borehole cameras and even an untested rescue capsule, scores of people were raised from their beds and pressed into service. 'We didn't know what to expect, but we knew that the guys didn't have that much time,' Louis Bartels said later.

Below ground, Blaine Mayhugh's hands were cut and bleeding as he and the other eight miners tried frantically to build a wall to stop the advancing tide of water. While some of the miners hurled cinder blocks atop each other to build the wall, Mayhugh and others slapped mud and grit into the gaps in a vain attempt to make it watertight. Still the water kept on coming, and with it foul air. At one point Mayhugh and John Unger vomited due to the combination of low oxygen, tiredness and tension. They were not the only ones in trouble. Pretty soon Tom Foy was once again complaining of chest pains. 'I'm leaving you guys, I think I'm having a heart attack,' he said, his voice hoarse with the effort of speaking. 'If you are, we all are,' someone replied in the gloom.

By now they could hear the drilling above them as the bit on Bartels's rig tore through the rock above. But the air was running out fast. As the sound of the drill grew louder and louder, their hearts beat faster and faster as they gasped for air. All were breathing hard through their mouths. Some were simply concentrating on trying to fill their lungs. One complained that his tongue was dry and his stomach cramping – both signs of extreme oxygen deprivation. They were literally down to their last few breaths.

Then suddenly the drill punched through, showering the men with rock and earth. Indeed, such was the accuracy of the drilling that John Unger later said that he had to leap out of the way as the 6-inch bit came through the shaft roof and rapidly dropped the remaining 4 feet to the floor. With the drill bit came the compressed-air pipe (which runs down the center of the drill shaft to blow rock chips, slurry and other detritus clear), which for the moment landed in a pool of water. One of the men grabbed it and let the good air wash over them, drawing it deep into their oxygen-starved lungs. It had arrived in the nick of time, the drill breaking through at 5.06, just as dawn was breaking. The drill team had taken just over 130 minutes to grind through 230 feet of rock and earth, a blistering pace at a shade under 2 feet per minute.

Above them, rescue workers shut down every piece of machinery, apart from the compressor, and prepared to listen for any sound from below. A member of the drill team hammered five times on the steel, and then Nicoletti quickly turned off the motors for a brief moment of silence to find out if they could hear anything in return. Suddenly, tapping came back through the steel – three distinct sequences of taps, it seemed: three times, then five times, and finally nine times. Not everyone was absolutely certain, but the sequence was significant. In miners' code, three taps is a universal signal that men are in danger, five taps means that they are barricaded in and cannot move, and nine taps signifies the number of men alive. 'That was our sign that our prayers had been answered,' said Louis Bartels. The mood at the command center a mile away was also lifted when Joe Sbaffoni, who was at the site, held up his phone to catch the sound from drill steel so that it could be heard at the other end. 'It was a sweet sound,' says John Urosek. 'We were excited and our sense of urgency went up tenfold. Now for sure we knew we had life down there. Whether it was one or nine, we were going to get them out.'

Under normal circumstances the drill and drill steels would have been taken out and hollow casings inserted to form a vertical pipe from the surface to the mine chamber. Then a telephone, camera, food, water, medical and other essential supplies would have been lowered down. Eventually a larger shaft would have been drilled close by and the men taken out through that. These, though, were not normal circumstances.

The euphoria in the command center was short lived. The rescuers faced two linked and virtually insuperable problems caused by the iron laws of physics. First, the trapped miners were at an elevation of 1,830 feet and the water in the Saxman mine was 35 feet above their heads at the 1,865-foot level, which meant that the level would continue to rise in Quecreek Number 1. Even though the rate of flooding had slowed from 200,000 gallons to around 70,000 gallons a minute, they knew that it was only a matter of time before the whole of the Quecreek mine was filled. Their best-guess estimate was that the water in Quecreek was at the 1,810-foot elevation – just 20 feet below the trapped miners. The men had perhaps an hour left before they were engulfed by the encroaching flood.

Second, the 6-inch shaft they had just drilled into the mine might actually hasten their deaths. There was a difference in air pressure between the surface and the mine floor. The air underground had been compressed by the inrushing water, which meant that if they pulled the drill out it would be like removing the valve in a car tire, letting the air hiss out. Not only would the air rush out from underground, but it would be followed by a spume of mine water under pressure, immediately extinguishing any pocket of air presently keeping the miners alive.

Kevin Stricklin was all too aware of the quandary they were in. 'It was inevitable that these guys were gonna drown if we didn't come up with something. I had no idea at the time of what to do. It was a bad situation to be in because I'd never heard tapping underground before [at previous mine accidents] and I'm thinking that we finally got some guys that are alive and they may end up drowning if we don't get to them immediately. You just felt so helpless.'

Everyone realized that they had at most sixty minutes in which to come up with a solution. One man, however, MSHA engineer John Urosek, had anticipated the problem while the drill team were at work. He suggested keeping the drill shaft in the mine and forcing compressed air into the shaft to create a 'bubble' of air under pressure that would stop the water rising further (the air pressure then being greater than the water pressure) as well as giving the men air to breathe. When he first gave voice to his theory there was some skepticism among his colleagues. What worked on paper might not work in a mine shaft. They needed to make some rapid calculations in order to see if Urosek's idea was practicable.

At the MSHA office in Hunker, Dr Kelvin Wu and his team were asked to work out the air pressure needed to keep the water at bay. In the meantime, the team at the drill site asked Louis Bartels about the capacity of the drill compressor he was using, and discovered that its maximum output was 350 pounds per square inch. Working frantically, Dr Wu estimated that air pressurized to 15 psi pumped in at a rate of 980 cubic feet per minute – well within the range of the compressor – would hold the water back, creating a survival bubble for the men. It was decided to double the pressure to 30 psi on the assumption that much of the air would leak from the hollow drill tube on its way to the trapped mine.

There was a second, critical, question. While the compressor had the necessary capacity, the crucial point was whether the pumped air would be fit for the men to breathe. From the command center, Gerry Davis checked with Bill Firtel, a technical expert at Consol Energy. He explained that there were three types of compressor – the good, the average and the ugly. The good was a high-pressure fan that pumped out ordinary clean air. The average was a rotary compressor that pushed out air that was combined with oily fumes from the machine, which were noxious but not life-threatening. The piston-engine-driven compressor that pumped out carbon monoxide and other deadly gases was the worst. If such a machine were to be used the air would kill the trapped miners in five minutes. Davis breathed a huge sigh of relief when he discovered that Louis

Bartels was using a rotary compressor. He also quizzed the driller about how long it would take to remove the drill and steels and insert a casing. Bartels told him that it would take at least ninety minutes, and probably two hours. As an added complication, the casing was too wide and would have had to be cut down. Since they only had an hour, that settled it. Urosek's brainchild was a go.

There was still one outstanding problem. A half-inch gap between the drill and the surrounding shaft meant that the good compressed air was being sucked out almost as soon as it hit the mine shaft. The gap had to be plugged, and fast. Urosek, whose idea had just earned him the nickname 'the Bubble Boy', called Joe Sbaffoni at the drill site. 'Joe, I don't care what you do or how you do it. But you have to plug the top of that hole.'

Sbaffoni, who is a volunteer fireman in his spare time, suddenly thought of using the airbags that fire trucks carry for use in car wrecks. He hustled over to the fire crews who had gathered with their engines along the county road and got them to work, inflating airbags and using them to plug gaps around the drill hole as best they could. They were showered with water and mud and sprayed with jets of air as they jammed the bags around the pipe to form a seal. Men were covered head to toe in mud driven out of the hole by the air pressure; it was hitting them so hard that it burnt their skin. But the seal held.

The 6-inch life-support system was in place.

In the gray light of early morning, as firemen and rescue workers wrestled with the jets of mud and water, Joe Kostyk and Ron Schad were wandering around their backyards. Neither had been able to sleep. Like the rest of the crew, they had come home exhausted at around four o'clock in the morning. When Schad tried to explain the events of the night to his wife Diana he was unable to say more than a few words before he burst into tears. Eventually he lay down on his bed, but when he closed his eyes all he could hear was Dennis Hall screaming his warning over the telephone, and the thunder of rushing water. He got up and went outside.

All of the nine men who had escaped were in the same state. No one could sleep. All they could think about was the water, the noise and the darkness and confusion, and the fate of their nine friends. They themselves had cheated death. Now they feared the worst for their buddies. Yet as Joe Kostyk expressed his deepest fears to his wife, she remained steadfast in her belief that the nine trapped men were alive. 'Have faith,' said Andrea, a devout Catholic. 'You have got to believe that they are alive. You have to believe in a miracle.'

Chapter V

'IS MY DADDY DEAD?'

THE WAITING WAS THE WORST OF IT. And the waiting was, for the most part, women's work. Endless minutes dragging into eternal hours. Not knowing what to think, except the worst. And the numbers spinning round and round in tired and anxious minds. What was it they said? Fifty million gallons of water? Hard to imagine, let alone to survive. Then, at last, the dark, nagging hours before dawn were over, the raw uncertainty ended. Their men were alive. Or so it seemed. The rescue team had heard tapping. Yet there were so many 'what ifs?' cascading through the fevered imaginations of those waiting above ground for news. What did the nine taps mean – nine men alive? Had the rescuers heard right? Could my man be missing, or is he injured? If so, how badly? And what about Dad? What about his weak heart? What about his medication?

All that water. Millions of gallons of it rushing underground. For a moment, when Leslie Mayhugh closed her eyes she could visualize the flood surging towards her husband Blaine and her father, Tom Foy. They would be helpless. In her imagination she saw them forced beneath the water, straining for breath, fighting for life in the swirling darkness. Their faces seemed so close that she could almost reach out and touch them.

With a start, she opened her eyes, looked round the room, saw the tight, set faces, the anxious eyes, and was back in the Sipesville fire hall. Back in the looming present. 'Did I turn my bath off?' she thought. 'Who can I get to feed Buddy [the family dog]?'

From domestic trivia to the awful probability that she would never see her husband or her father ever again; the last few hours had been an endless loop of self-reproach, confusion and aching despair. It was her fault, of course – or so she told herself. If only she had kissed Blaine before he left for the mine; if only she worked longer hours at the nursing home so that he didn't have to work so hard; if only he had stayed in the Navy; if only . . . She should have noticed the omens. The uncertainty, the dragging fear and sense of impending doom, enveloped her heart like a dark cloak, plunging her into the depths of despair. Then the diminutive brunette would curl up in a ball, rocking back and forth in her chair, occasionally moaning and sobbing.

At other times she would take a picture of Blaine and Tom from a pocket in her sweatshirt. It showed her men together in happier days, arms round each other's shoulders, all smiles during a successful fishing trip. Seeing them like that was a further cause for tears. The only time the glimmer of a smile passed Leslie's lips was when someone suggested that Blaine, who had wanted to be a Navy SEAL, would have been lifting up the much shorter Tom in the tunnels to save him from the water.

'The only way I can describe her behavior is watching someone who is in labor,' recalls her friend Kathy Engle, who joined the Foy and Mayhugh families in their vigil at the Sipesville fire hall at breakfast time on Thursday, 25 July. 'It was awful to see her that way. She was in so much pain, her body jerking like she was having a spasm.'

By then nine hours had passed since that awful phone call. Nine hours of not knowing for certain that the men were alive, despite the news from the drill site. Inevitably, perhaps, John Weir, as the representative of the mine, was firmly in the firing line as families took out their fears and frustrations on him. During the first long, anxious night John Phillippi's wife Melissa had, in Weir's words, 'cleaned his clock' about the paucity of information flowing from those in charge of the rescue operation. She demanded an end to what she called 'the bullshit'. Weir, who promised to tell the families only what he knew to be true because he had seen or heard it, was doing his best in an impossible situation. For some, though, his briefings were never enough. 'It's driving us all nuts not knowing what is going on,' complained Ashley Popernack, Mark's cousin. Even so, the information was a huge advance over the old days, when mine companies would deliberately keep accidents quiet, knowing that crowds made rescue work more difficult. The sight of distraught women running through the streets of Pennsylvania mining towns, desperate for information about their loved ones, is one that those who witnessed it will never forget.

Certainly Kathy Engle and Karen Schafer will always remember the scene that greeted them as they hugged and kissed their friend Leslie Mayhugh, her mother Denise and Leslie's sisters Tonya, Tracey and Amy. Blaine's family were bewildered and shocked, struggling to grasp the enormity of what had happened. 'Oh it's awful, they don't know what to do, don't even know where they are,' Denise Foy moaned, struggling to maintain her composure.

Outside the sun was shining, but in the hall the mood was somber, conversation subdued, the families colonizing different parts of the room for themselves. When a cell phone shrilled, all heads would swivel, just as they did when someone burst into tears. In the first few hours the atmosphere in the fire hall had the awkwardness of a dentist's waiting room. While the trapped men, like all miners, saw themselves as members of a close-knit brotherhood, that sense of belonging, of community, was absent among their women. In the old days of company mining towns the wives and mothers would have known every other family intimately, but that no longer applies today. Separated geographically, most had only met each other at the company's annual Christmas party or the occasional company picnic.

As a result, for most of the long night Sue Ellen Unger had been on her own, sitting quietly in her wheelchair. Other families felt sorry that she was so alone, but she impressed everyone with her quiet serenity, always smiling, always confident. 'I know they are going to come out,' she would say to those who, overcoming their diffidence, approached her. Her Christian faith was her guide and her comforter through the long vigil, and by early morning she had been joined by numerous parishioners from the church where she and John worshiped.

Just as she had behaved when she was first diagnosed with multiple sclerosis, Sue Ellen displayed an inner resilience throughout, a matter-of-fact optimism that everything would turn out for the best. 'She was simply an inspiration,' said her friend Rona Hemminger. Nor was she the only one. Right from the start Randy Fogle's sister-in-law, Laurie Yoder, impressed many people as someone with an uncanny knack for lifting someone up just when they were feeling down. 'We have to have faith,' she would say. 'They are going to be all right.'

Others, like Cathy Hileman, found comfort in the power of prayer, while Robert Pugh's staunchly Catholic parents, Robert Sr and Mary, were comforted by their priest, Father Martin Breski, praying frequently to Saint Anthony of Padua, the patron saint of lost articles. They and other parishioners took it as a sign that relics of Saint Margaret Mary, which were being flown from the Vatican to Canada for the Pope's visit, ended up in West Pennsylvania and, for various reasons, remained in the area for the next few days.

During that first night and the early part of the following morning everyone in the fire hall seemed to be on a roller-coaster, hoping for the best but fearing the worst. For a little while the atmosphere might brighten, and then someone would mutter, 'They're dead. I know they are dead,' and once again the funereal mood would descend, the low buzz of conversation punctuated by the sound of sobbing.

Understandably, it was the women with young children who found the ordeal the hardest to bear. Like Leslie Mayhugh, Sandy Popernack, the mother of two young boys, Luke and Dan, was often in tears, unable to stop herself from fearing the worst for her husband Mark. 'She was a nervous wreck,' recalled Robin Zambanini, who spent her time consoling families in between preparing food for the growing army. 'She was in tears most of the time and nothing you did seemed to calm her down.'

The sight of their children, and the thought that they might never see their fathers again, proved to be virtually unbearable. Then there were the questions from the young ones, asking when Daddy was coming home and if he was OK. At around nine o'clock on that first dreadful morning, young Tyler Mayhugh was subdued and pensive, clearly fretting about his father. He approached his mother and the rest of the Foy women and asked plaintively, 'Is my daddy dead? Is he gonna die?'

As Karen Schafer, herself the mother of three teenage daughters, recalled, 'It pulled the heart right out of your chest.' Yet, even though she was in so much pain herself, Leslie was always positive but honest with her children, explaining to them that mining was dangerous and that everyone was working hard to bring Daddy home safely. Tyler's second question, though, was one that no one in the room could answer.

At that moment, neither could his father. For a time Blaine and his colleagues had huddled near the 6-inch pipe, the compressed air warming and sustaining them. Even more important was the feeling that although they were trapped in this dark, wet

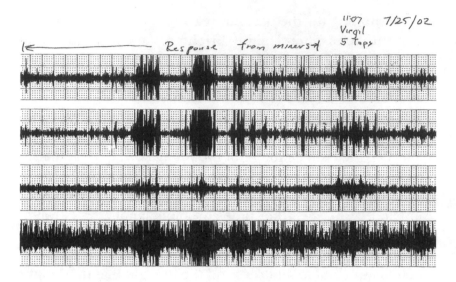

The seismograph readings that indicated the men were still alive (MSHA)

place, they were no longer isolated, and that others knew that they were there and were working to free them. Every ten minutes or so they would bang on the pipe to signal to the rescuers that they were still alive. At around 11.00 in the morning they heard the distinctive pinging of a seismograph down the pipe. Whenever they heard a ping they pounded back nine times and five times, the graph paper used by the seismograph distinctly recording the sound that signified the men were alive. 'It was an exciting time,' recalls John Urosek who, with Dr Kravitz and Virgil Brown, conducted the test. While this fresh evidence gave rescuers and families alike renewed hope that all the men were alive, they could not have begun to appreciate the deadly predicament the nine miners faced that morning. The only clue was when, at midday on Thursday, they tried to make further contact, there seemed to be no response to the ping from the seismograph.

With the water rising inexorably towards them, however, the miners were forced to retreat. Eventually they moved several hundred feet from the air shaft to a point close to Entry Number 1, all the while desperately building barricades of mud and cinderblocks behind them to keep back the advancing tide. From time to time they would pound on the roof with Robert Pugh's hammer in case a rescuer with listening gear was trying to get a fix on their position.

That morning they built five walls, known as stoppings, as they had been taught to do during their safety training. Each time a wall was complete, however, the rising water would slop over the top, rendering it useless. By the time they started building the sixth, the rising tide had already reached them. In these moments it seemed to the nine trapped men that Fate was toying with their lives, deliberating as to whether they should live or die. 'It was plain hell, buddy,' was how Robert Pugh would later describe these desperate hours. By around midday on Thursday – Blaine Mayhugh was the only one with a watch – they were confined to a long, narrow area measuring perhaps 18 by 60 feet, and with a roof height of barely 5 feet. Only Tom Foy could stand more or less upright, and then only with difficulty. They had nowhere left to retreat to. 'Death was staring me in the face and it was coming to get me,' recalled Ron Hileman. 'There was nothing to do but stand there and let death come and get us.' As the water advanced, Foy prayed for deliverance.

The crew boss, Randy Fogle, ordered his men not to look at the advancing water, but most did. Then for a minute or two they would fall silent. It was about 70 feet away and creeping towards them fast. 'Where is it?' someone asked. Fogle replied, 'It's coming.' He guessed that they had an hour, then it would be all up for them. 'We thought we had drawn our last card there,' admitted Mark Popernack, who had already cheated death twice during the night.

At this time of almost unbearable mental torture, the men thought of their wives and their families. Blaine Mayhugh borrowed a pen from his boss, tore a piece of cardboard from a box of resin used by roof bolters, and wrote a final message to his family, telling them how much he loved them and that he would see them again one day in Heaven. He passed the pen round, and one by one they all wrote brief notes of love, regret and affection which they placed in a dirty white plastic lunch pail. Fogle sealed the airtight lid and lashed the pail to a rock, so that it might be found one day, when the mine was eventually reopened and drained. For men of few words, these were sentiments so raw, so painful and so private that even today they will not allow their partners to read the letters, let alone discuss them in public.

For a while afterwards they were silent, each man wrapped in his own thoughts. Then Tom Foy said that if they were going to die, they should at least die together, brothers to the last. He grabbed a plastic-coated 3/16-inch cable and lashed it round himself, then began to pass the free end through the belts of the other miners. In this way their bodies would not be scattered through the mine. John Unger and Mark Popernack decided to wait until the water was nearer before tying themselves to their friends. Cross-grained as ever, Dennis Hall refused point blank to join them. When the time came, his plan was to try to find a way into the Saxman mine or, failing that, to take a last breath, dive into the flood and come up at a place where the water touched the roof, so that he would drown quickly. The last thing he wanted to hear before the end was the sound of his friends choking to death.

It was now that Blaine Mayhugh suddenly asked what was the best way to drown. 'Do you let yourself go under water, do you fight it, or what?' he said. No one knew the answer. It was not really a question anyway, simply a way of putting his fear into words. This was, he thought, no way to die – cold, wet and hunched over in the dark, hundreds of feet underground.

At another point, Blaine asked John Unger, the crew's unofficial chaplain, whether he could go to Heaven even though he had not been baptized. It was an unconscious echo of his wife's own thoughts expressed to her friends just a couple of weeks before. 'Good people go to Heaven no matter what,' Unger told him.

Then they settled down to wait in the darkness, with the sound of the water that would engulf them coming ever closer. They thought of their families, of others they loved, and they prayed. One of the nine began to recite the words of the Lord's Prayer. Then another picked it up, then all of them, and in the darkness they spoke the words which, down the centuries, have brought such comfort at times of dire peril. Yet they could not help imagining the shudder of fear when the advancing water first brushed their boots, then slowly rose up their legs and bodies. And then, finally, the darkness.

It was only a matter of time – and not much time, at that.

Time was the one commodity the men in the command center could not buy at any price. They guessed that the decision to create a bubble of air for the trapped miners had won them breathing space, both literally for the nine men underground, and figuratively for the rescue operation. But not much. For although the technique looked good on paper, it had never actually been used before in all America's long mining history. What the rescue planners knew for certain was that the water level was only a few feet below where the men were trapped, and that it was rising fast. In the light of that knowledge, they decided to use the tried and tested technique of pumping water from the mine to buy them a few hours' grace.

During the night, two high-capacity pumps had been hauled deep into the mine by the men of the night shift, who worked frantically to hook up the pumps and organize a power supply to them. By around six in the morning, the gush from the Saxman mine into Quecreek Number 1 had slowed from 200,000 to around 70,000 gallons a minute – but that was still a flow rate far beyond the capacity of any mine in America to cope with. At the 1,820-foot level – 10 feet below where the men were trapped – the rescue workers decided to make their final stand. They were 1,000 feet inside the mine, ready to do battle with the floodwaters.

It proved to be no contest. Within minutes the pumps, the hoses and the power center had been engulfed by water. The miners working deep within Quecreek Number 1 were forced to beat a hasty retreat, and now feared the worst. 'We thought the other guys were goners,' recalled Eric Brant, who had been on the shift before the flood. 'I was counting my own blessings when I saw that water coming at us.' The sheer weight of water was daunting for everyone. 'It was like pissing in the wind,' Kevin Stricklin remembers, with a shake of his head. 'This wasn't like some little pump. This was a substantial effort.' For a time, then, on that first morning not one drop of water was being pumped out of the mine. It was during these hours that the waters rose so rapidly towards the trapped men. By lunchtime on Thursday, as the nine miners waited for the end, the floodwater was at the mouth of the mine and rising so quickly that by mid-afternoon it came within 4 inches of the top of a 16-foot-high garage door outside the entrance. 'When I saw water in the mouth of the pit my heart was sinking,' admits Gerry Davis. 'It's a hell of a feeling knowing you have nine men down there.'

In the meantime, frantic efforts were under way to locate sites at which boreholes could be drilled into the mine in order to pump water out. The survey teams were guided by one over-riding principle: nothing must be done that might puncture the air bubble surrounding the miners. Using the most up-to-date technology, Bob Long and Sean Isgan had worked throughout the night with their GPS apparatus system to find sites above ground corresponding to water-filled areas of the mine below. Their brief was to make a survey and locate on the

surface six positions from which holes could be drilled success-
fully into the mine. It eventually turned out that five out of the
six boreholes were precisely on the target, the drills powering
straight into the water. Ironically, the only one that missed –
despite the drillers subsequently dynamiting the hole – was due
to human error: the underground coordinates had been taken
down incorrectly.

While they were working with their laptop and GPS, all night
and into the early morning drill companies throughout the
state and beyond were dragooned into service, the call going
out for drills that could drive 300 feet down into the earth to
provide the necessary boreholes. Companies involved in well-
drilling raced to the scene to offer their help. As just one example, workers for Wayne's Water 'n' Wells in Somerset County
first heard of the trapped miners from the TV news. They sent
along their drilling equipment, including a massive 6-ton
barracks pump along with an eight-man crew and two rig
tenders. As Gerry Davis put it, 'The whole county came alive.'
By lunchtime on Thursday there was a traffic jam at the mine as
pumps large and small arrived.

The most urgent need, though, was for a superdrill that
could bore a 30-inch-diameter hole down to the trapped men.
This would provide a shaft large enough to take the 22-inch
yellow-painted metal rescue capsule, needed to transport the
trapped men to safety, which was being rushed from Beckley, in
the neighboring state West Virginia. Even this was a gamble.
The thirty-year-old capsule had never been used in a real-life
rescue.

As it turned out, a drilling operation run by a father-and-son
team, Gene and Duane Yost, had just such a formidable drill bit,
weighing a whopping 1,500 pounds, heavier than a small car.
From his home in Greene County, south of Pittsburgh, Gene
Yost explained to rescue workers that there was one major
problem. The bit was near by, but the 46-foot high rig needed to

grind it into the earth was on another job in Clarksburg, West Virginia. Even with the escort readily promised by the police, it was going to take hours to bring it on site.

None the less, the delay did give the rescue team time to prepare the site, to lay down a makeshift rock road, a concrete-and-rock base for the massive drill rig, and a steel-encased entry hole so that drilling could begin the moment the rig was set up. 'It takes time to set the casing,' observed Joe Gallo, the PBS mine engineer who played a vital part in the operation. 'It takes time to set the rig in place. It takes time to set up all the air compressors that the rig requires. It's agonizing. The time just seemed to crawl. It seemed like it took forever to do anything with those guys under there waiting for us. Seconds seem like hours.'

Once again, local contacts proved to be invaluable in minimizing delays. While an excavator dug down into the soft earth, Sipesville's volunteer fire chief, Mark Zambanini, who works full-time as a payloader for an asphalt company, New Enterprise Stone and Lime, contacted his bosses and explained the gravity and urgency of the miners' predicament. For a start, he said, the rescuers needed 500 tons of rock, 100 cubic yards of concrete and 30 feet of 36-inch-diameter pipe to prepare the site for the superdrill. 'You got it,' he was told. New Enterprise even halted a planned concrete pour on the Pennsylvania Turnpike that morning and diverted the trucks to the rescue site. 'Lives are more important than roads,' Zambanini was told. Gratefully, he agreed.

Escorted by police cruisers with their sirens blaring, a five-truck convoy carrying the drill rig arrived from West Virginia at 2.30 on Thursday afternoon. When the news was announced to the families and friends waiting at the fire hall, it was greeted with cheers. At last things were moving.

Nothing in this rescue was as simple as it seemed, however. The arrival of the drill rig, which it would take five hours to set up, only highlighted the difficulties facing the men coordinating the rescue. The air bubble had saved the lives of the trapped miners. As far as the rescuers knew, it was keeping the flood-water at bay as well as providing them with reasonably fresh air. Like scuba divers, though, they were living in a pressurized envi-ronment, several times the pressure on the surface. There was a very real risk that if they were brought up the rescue shaft they would succumb to decompression sickness, commonly known as 'the bends'. This condition, which can result in blindness, paralysis, convulsions and even death, is caused by prolonged exposure to an environment in which the ambient pressure is higher than normal atmospheric pressure. The longer a diver stays underwater (where the pressure increases with the depth) the more nitrogen dissolves in his or her blood. If the diver ascends too rapidly, the dissolved nitrogen comes out of solu-tion too quickly and forms bubbles in the body's blood and tissues, resulting in severe pain. Normally divers decompress their bodies by slowly rising from the depths at which they were operating, stopping on the way for defined periods of time, or spend time in a decompression chamber if they ascend quickly, where they breathe a mixture of helium and oxygen in varying proportions. For the miners, subjected to high ambient air pres-sures, neither was a workable option. The moment the rescue drill broke through the roof of the mine the pressure seal would be broken and they would be at risk.

As a result, the problem that now presented itself to the res-cuers was how to bring the men to the surface through the res-cue shaft without killing them. The nearest equivalent was rescuing a sailor from a submarine that has either sunk or which, for whatever reason, cannot surface normally. In such a case the escaping sailor has to go from the submarine, main-tained more or less at atmospheric pressure, through an air lock into water at a much higher pressure, which decreases as he rises to the surface. For the rescuers at Quecreek, however, such an operation was far beyond their experience. The solution the mining experts hit upon was to call in another expert.

Dr Richard Kunkle is the cofounder, with paramedic Danny Sacco, of the Special Medical Response Team (SMRT), a 'lean, mean and mobile' outfit designed to go where other health teams fear to tread. Established twenty years ago in Homer City, Pennsylvania, to assist underground in mine emergencies, SMRT has gone on to provide vital support at disasters around the world. The men and women of SMRT have played a vital role in incidents as diverse as earthquakes in Armenia and the Philippines to ice storms in upstate New York as well as the 9/11 atrocity in New York City. So when the Quecreek mine flooded, the group was one of the first to be contacted by the Somerset County 911 communications center and was on the scene by midnight on Wednesday, 24 July. For the first few hours they felt helpless, unable to apply their medical expertise as no one knew whether this was to be a rescue or a recovery operation.

The sound of tapping at dawn was the call for SMRT to swing into action. They alerted the mine-rescue command center to the clinical dangers associated with long periods living under pressure, and warned that unless steps were taken, the miners might well die from the bends even as they were being rescued. With water still pouring into the mine, it was now imperative to find a way to bring the men out of the mine under pressure, and then somehow decompress them at the surface. The problem was thrown at Dr Kunkle, a calm and softly spoken trauma specialist, who, in conjunction with mine engineers, immediately began to work feverishly to come up with a solution.

After a morning spent surfing the web and calling engineering companies, as well as organizations like Divers' Alert Network, the Society of Undersea Medicine and the US Navy, it became apparent to Kunkle and his helpers that there was no device available that could keep the miners under pressure while they were being lifted from the mine. 'It left a lot of people around the country scratching their heads,' Dr Kunkle observes wryly. As a result, they were left with only one option: they would have to design and build any such device on site. Kunkle, together with a local drilling engineer, Larry Neff – described as a young J. F. Kennedy lookalike – sat down with a sheaf of scrap computer paper and a white 3-by-5 notepad, and tried to sketch out a design for a workable pressure chamber in which, one by one, the trapped men could be brought to the surface.

Although the techniques of transferring people between differing pressures are not technologically difficult – after all, men have worked in space for decades, and underwater for much longer – they have never been used in mining. The rescue team needed to be able to bring a miner to the surface and transfer him to a decompression chamber without losing the life-providing pressure needed by the other miners still below. At the same time, any device they constructed would have to be able to accommodate the drill, its hammer and a tool steel, because when the drill broke through to the miners there would be no chance of removing the machinery without breaking the pressure seal at the surface. These last pieces would have to be removed in Dr Kunkle's pressure chamber while it was sealed off from the shaft. In addition, the chamber would have to be equipped with a means to allow the rescue capsule to be raised into it, and then lowered back down the shaft from inside it, as well as a means of sealing off its base from the pressurized shaft while the rescued miner was taken out.

Several hours and uncountable pieces of crumpled paper later, Kunkle and Neff had sketched what turned out to be a unique device, 40 feet high and 3 feet in diameter, which fulfilled all these criteria. It was effectively a huge cylindrical seal designed to be bolted over the hole, equipped with two airtight doors, one at the side and one, a sliding device, at the bottom, which would permit entry and exit without compromising the pressure inside the rescue shaft. There was a 2-inch hole in the top fitted with a tough oil-control seal, which would allow the rescue capsule's cable to slide through it without any loss of pressure in the chamber. Finally, a valve was added through which compressed air would be pumped to maintain or increase the pressure inside. By late afternoon on Thursday, they had a workable design. Then, having secured the agreement of the MSHA experts in charge, they had to get it built. Neff, who is the construction supervisor at BethEnergy Mines Inc. in Revloc in Cambria County, reached into his contact book and called another father-and-son team, Don and Buddy Walker, who operate Lincoln Contracting in nearby Boswell. Working at the drill site from the roughed-out plans, the Walkers' team shaped and welded metal plates to the required size and configuration. In just six hours they had completed the job. As Neff and Kunkle inspected the finished work by torchlight on Thursday night they found only a couple of tiny gaps that would let out air, easily combated by pumping in compressed air. The module was to all intents and purposes airtight, a remarkable piece of engineering and design in the time available. 'Everyone stepped up to the plate,' observes Dr Kunkle modestly.

While Kunkle was working on the rescue module, his SMRT colleague, Dr Nick Colovos, a diver with the US Navy Reserve, was contacting diving experts at the US Navy's base in Norfolk, Virginia. He had two questions: what was the maximum time available to transfer a man from the rescue capsule to a decompression chamber without ill effects; and, by the way, did they have nine portable decompression chambers they could lend the rescuers? The answers were fifteen minutes, and yes. Would the Navy cooperate? Yes, given the necessary authority. State and federal agencies were consulted about the overall cost of the operation, and these in turn called Pennsylvania's Governor, Mark Schweiker, who had been kept fully up to date with events at Quecreek. 'Guys, don't waste your time calling me about expenditures,' he told them. 'Deploy. Send in everything you have got. Time is of the essence.'

As a result, by mid-afternoon, a convoy of trucks carrying ten decompression chambers – the largest number ever assembled for an inland rescue – together with a unit of Navy SEALs, rolled out of the huge Virginia Navy base, escorted by state troopers. Within seven hours they were on site, a very welcome addition to the growing rescue efforts. With some trepidation, Dr Kunkle and Larry Neff showed the new arrivals their brainchild. It was looked over approvingly by the Navy experts. 'Jeez, this should work,' admitted Captain Henry Schwartz, who suggested only that they put a pressure valve on the module alongside the existing pressure gauge.

The arrival of the Navy SEALs once again triggered the debate inside the command center about the merits or otherwise of using divers to rescue the miners. The idea was quickly ruled out as virtually impossible, especially when the Navy experts explained that not only would a diver have to find his way through a maze of flooded mine shafts, but that in addition to all his gear he would have to carry three tanks of air, two for his own use and one for each miner he brought back. The risks were far too high for the plan to be considered seriously.

The loan and transportation of Navy divers and decompression chambers did not come cheap. In the space of just forty-eight hours an estimated $6 million-worth of equipment was on site, and almost from the beginning of the rescue local politicians had weighed in with their 10 cents' worth. Early on Thursday morning, an aide to the local Congressman, John Murtha, showed up at the site wanting to know how he could help. Gerry Davis spent thirty minutes briefing him. After his aide had reported back to him, Congressman Murtha suggested that they brought in the Federal Emergency Management Agency (FEMA), which normally deals with hurricanes, forest fires and other natural disasters, to coordinate the rescue. Although well meant, the idea met with a chilly response. Inevitably it would have led to FEMA, which has little, if any, experience with mines, taking over responsibility for the rescue from the Mine Safety and Health Administration, the very people who were most experienced in mining disasters. Fortunately Murtha dropped the idea, leaving the experts to get on with the job.

If local politicians were eager to use their contacts to move matters along, it was the arrival of Governor Mark Schweiker at the rescue site early on Thursday afternoon that set the mood of optimism and cooperation in the face of an as yet very uncertain outcome, a mood that was to become such a marked feature of the operation. Over the next three days he was to become the public face of the rescue effort, committed heart and soul to its success. His adoption of the 'nine for nine' baseball slogan – expressing not just the hope, but the belief that all the men would come out alive – became first a local, and then a national, mantra. In the process Schweiker became, for a time, one of the most recognizable political figures in America, earning laudatory comparison with New York's Mayor Rudy Giuliani, who had rallied the city after terrorist outrages of 9/11. An early call from the Governor to the White House set the tone. When he asked President Bush for assistance, he received the unequivocal answer, 'Anything you want, you got it.' And that included the US Navy, with its huge resources and vast technical expertise. The USN had said that all it needed to cooperate with the rescue was the requisite authority. There was no higher authority in the land.

Although Governor Schweiker had been kept closely informed of developments from the start by David Hess, the Secretary of Pennsylvania's Department of Environmental Protection (which includes the Deep Mine Safety Bureau), it was his meeting with the families at Sipesville fire hall on Thursday afternoon which brought home to the forty-nine-year-old father of three the human cost of the drama. Despite the phalanx of mine officials accompanying him, most of the families had no idea who he was when he walked in, dressed in jeans and a casual shirt. They thought he was just a good-looking guy who smiled more than most. 'Folks, this is a rescue operation. Put your faith and heart and hands into it and we can succeed,' he told them when he rose to address them, sensing the fragile mood within the hall. He assured them that the superdrill would be working soon, and promised that it would not be too long before they saw their loved ones again. Afterwards, he told Bob Pugh's parents that he would do his best to enable their grandson, Bob's son, Ben, a professional golfer who was stranded in Scotland at a tournament at St Andrew's, to fly home 'as a matter of urgency'. He kept his word.

While the Governor's sentiments were undoubtedly sincere, there were those in his audience at the fire hall that day who found him rather patronizing and awkward. He seemed to be disconcerted by having to speak without a script, although at future meetings they began, almost instinctively, to warm to a man who clearly had their best interests at heart. Certainly his easy manner and willingness to roll up his sleeves impressed the rescue workers when he visited the drill site. 'Put your heart and souls and hands into it,' he told them, using much the same phrase that he had spoken to the families. Later, when he spotted two drillers, filthy and exhausted after working round the clock, he handed them the key to his hotel room and told them, 'You need a shower. Go get a shower and get some rest.' Gestures like that endeared him to the rescuers who saw him as one of their own. 'I think most governors would have come and looked over the guard rails and said, "Keep me informed, boys." Not this one,' remarked Sipesville's fire chief, Mark Zambanini. 'He jumped out of the car, walked right through the drill slurry and mud, and patted the boys on the back and told them they were doing a good job. He never seemed to leave. At three in the morning you would hear the sirens [of the police escort] and here would come the Governor again.'

Whatever the setbacks, in the coming days Schweiker maintained an upbeat note throughout. On Thursday, a short time after seeing the families, he found himself on more familiar territory, surrounded by reporters and TV camera crews at the hastily appointed media center, formerly the site of a Giant Eagle supermarket. Flanked by DEP Secretary David Hess and engineer Joe Sbaffoni he told the assembled journalists, 'We believe it is going well. They [the people involved in the rescue] are going feverishly. That drill . . . represents the opportunity to live.' Secretary Hess was more guarded, admitting that, 'It's a very ticklish situation we're in, very touch-and-go.'

Almost as ticklish was the situation Joe Sbaffoni found himself in. Along with Schweiker, he would find himself propelled into the national, and then the international spotlight over the next few days as the tale of the trapped miners began to seize audiences around the world, his pale, bespectacled face becoming a familiar sight to TV viewers as he explained the technical details of the rescue. Initially, he was a reluctant spokesman, scarcely able to conceal that he would much prefer to have a hands-on-role in the rescue. Yet when he objected to playing the part of spokesman, Hess told him, 'I'm your boss. You are coming with me.' From now on Sbaffoni was doing little to help drive the rescue bus, instead becoming the tour guide, albeit a much praised one, for the information-starved media, who were not only kept away from the rescue site, but also from the Sipesville fire hall where the trapped miners' families were gathered.

In truth, those families had enough to deal with without the attentions of the press. Some moments were better than others, however. While the Governor's visit had been well-intentioned, what really boosted morale was when, later the same afternoon, the families were taken to the rescue site to see for themselves exactly what efforts were being made to save their men. The sight that greeted them was a scene of organized chaos, teams of men straining to set up the giant rig for the superdrill, welders hammering on steel plate, trucks unloading equipment and supplies, and excavators packing earth around the casing at the mouth of the rescue shaft. In the background was the continual roar of the compressor, forcing air 240 feet down to their stranded menfolk.

In some ways, recognizing the reality of the situation was as difficult for the rescue workers as it had been for the miners' wives and families. Up until now the men below ground had been nameless victims to the rescuers. Now they saw not just the human toll on the families; many of them also realized that they knew the trapped men. Driller John 'Buck' Hamilton admitted that he found the long hours of work at the site less stressful than seeing the hopeful but anxious faces of the wives. One woman hugged him and said, 'Don't give up, guys.' As he asked later, 'What do you say to somebody like that?'

Bill Arnold couldn't believe his eyes when he saw his wife Lori with her arms around Sandy Popernack. He had known her and Mark for fifteen years, before they had even met each other. He grew up with Sandy, rode with her on the school bus every day, and went with her to the county fairs. 'It was tough seeing her,' he recalled, 'knowing that Mark was down there.'

It was tough, too, for Mark Popernack's eldest son Dan, aged ten. Initially reluctant to visit the rescue site he slowly came closer to the police line and watched intently as the men worked to set up the drill rig. Doug Custer's wife Cathy, who had been helping at the fire hall and went to the site with the families, sensed the boy's resentment toward his father. 'Dan, you must be really mad at your dad right now,' she said. He nodded in reply. She suggested that when Mark got out he could make it up to Dan by treating the two boys. 'Suggest something you like,' she said. After some initial hesitation he thought of trips to Caddy Shack, to the Seven Springs resort and to Pizza Hut.

Since his father hates pizza, this was an especially delicious form of retribution. Dan wrote his three wishes on his hand in felt-tip pen, ready to show his father. Cathy's ploy had the desired effect. For the first time that day the boy smiled.

During the visit to the site Leslie Mayhugh found herself consoling the rescue workers, making jokes to cheer them up. One worker was visibly shaken when he realized he knew some of the men who were trapped. Lowering his head, he said, 'You've got to be kidding. Not Blaine and Tom.' Leslie tried to make light of their predicament. Knowing that the rescue capsule was 22 inches wide, and that her father's waist was around 36 inches, she quipped, 'Now boys, you've got to grease my dad like a pig to get him out.'

For the trapped miners' families, strung out on adrenalin, anxiety and caffeine, it was a brief interlude of levity in a day of unbearable tension. Father Jack O'Malley saw something of the mood as he drove from Pittsburgh to Sipesville to help comfort the people in the fire hall. When he arrived at the turnpike toll-booth in Somerset, he found the woman attendant in tears because she knew some of those involved. Yet although many in the fire hall were assailed by strong doubts, equally powerful was the collective strength of faith, a characteristic of the community that profoundly affected O'Malley. 'I was impressed by the positive attitude of so many people. People were talking about a rescue rather than a recovery although I'm sure it was in the backs of many minds.'

By nightfall, most had adapted a little to the new reality of their lives, the tedious, tiring rhythms of waiting, treading the emotional tightrope between hope and despair, hysteria and calm. The rising water in the mine was always on their minds, even though the pumps were now beginning to make some headway. Many wives who had not eaten since daybreak, both out of solidarity with their menfolk trapped below and from a lack of appetite, now succumbed to the endlessly proffered plates of donuts, home-made sandwiches and snacks. Such was the avalanche of donated foodstuffs appearing at the fire hall that an appeal was made for local people to stop bringing perishable goods. As one priest joked, 'I probably put on five pounds in those three days.'

By that evening everyone in the fire hall was preparing to camp there for the night, either in their cars, in the hall or under the stars. Leslie Mayhugh surprised her family when she agreed to join her friends on a shopping trip to the nearest Walmart to buy blankets, toiletries and other essentials for the night ahead. When she asked the store for a discount, the staff gave her everything without charge. More importantly, however, her family took the fact that she made the trip to the store as a sign that this normally bubbly, fun-loving young woman was coming out of her initial shock. She even collapsed in fits of laughter when her friend Kathy Engle told of her own shock when she inadvertently put her hand on Denise Foy's false teeth, which had fallen out while she was dozing in the back of her Blazer. Leslie's mother, however, was not amused.

Other wives and family members reacted differently to the predicament in which everyone now found themselves. John Phillippi's wife Melissa, known as 'Missy', became a permanent fixture at the rescue site, maintaining a vigil close to the rescue shaft. She refused all pleas to return to the fire hall. 'It would have taken a bulldozer to move her,' Bill Arnold commented. 'She got here and refused to leave.' Hour after remorseless hour she sat there waiting, lost in her thoughts, oblivious to the people around her.

Missy and the other wives were not the only ones waiting. After an hour Blaine Mayhugh looked at his watch, its face backlit at the press of a button. Where was the water? For an hour they had held their collective breath, willing the water to stay back, praying for it to do so. It seemed as though those prayers had been answered. There was one tiny pocket of Quecreek mine that hadn't been flooded – and they were standing in it. Just to make sure, crew chief Randy Fogle drove a stick into the mud to mark the water's limit, and then tied a light bulb to it to act as a bobber in case the flood rose again. It didn't. The water stayed where it was, black, malevolent, but unmoving. Outside, at around the same time, late afternoon, mine officials noted that the water had stopped near the top of the garage hard by the mine entrance. This was to be the high-water mark of the flood.

So certain of dying, convinced that they had played their last card, almost resigned to their fate, it took some minutes for the trapped men to realize that they had a fighting chance of staying alive. And fight they would. They found a piece of ventilation canvas – in the old days miners' wives would dye these cloths and use them to make curtains – and laid it across the mud and the stones. They had been prepared to die together, now they huddled together to save their lives, desperately trying to keep warm in the chill 55-degree temperature, made worse by the fact that they were soaked. Blaine Mayhugh, ever the keep-fit fanatic, even started doing push-ups in the dark in an attempt to keep warm, to the ribald amusement of the rest of the crew. At around 7.30 in the evening they began to hear noises above them, and realized that a drill was pushing through the earth and rock towards them. If they could hang on, perhaps for twelve hours or maybe a little longer, then they would have a chance. After all they had gone through, that was all they asked for. A chance. Another roll of the dice.

For long periods they sat in darkness to save the batteries on their lamps. Every so often, however, two of them would turn on their cap lamps and go to check the water, which was still uncomfortably close. Mark Popernack was especially proud of his careful husbandry during his solitary wait while he was separated from the others, as the battery for his cap lamp easily lasted the longest. Every ten minutes or so they pounded on the roof to let their rescuers know that they were still alive. As yet there was no chance of getting back to the air pipe – there was still too much water – but by late evening Fogle reckoned that the level was going down. So did technicians at the command center as they realized that two huge diesel pumps, which could suck 20,000 gallons of water a minute from the mine and had roared into life on Thursday evening, were now making a difference. The news raised a cheer at the fire hall – and, later, across the land as millions sat glued to their TVs, willing the miners to survive. A prayer chain wrapped itself around all the churches of Somerset County.

No one was praying harder for rescue than the nine men trapped below ground. They could hear the drill biting its inexorable way towards them. At just after 9.00 their families were told that it had pushed 45 feet into the earth in around two hours. Those taking notes worked out the math and agreed with the Governor's prediction that the drill would be through to the miners shortly before dawn. They went to bed exhausted, but hopeful.

Down below, the men rested fitfully, grabbing ten minutes' sleep at a stretch on the rubble-strewn floor. The noise of the approaching drill was hardly conducive to rest. Not that they cared. Then there was silence. Blaine looked at the back-lit face of his watch. It was 1.30 in the morning. 'Maybe they've knocked off for the night,' he joked hopefully.

More than 200 feet above him, driller Duane Yost was calling the command center. 'Control, we've got a problem.'

Chapter VI

THE WAITING GAME

THEY CAME TO CALL THEM 'downdates': the times when the mine owner's representative, John Weir, and assorted mine officials stalked into the fire hall to deliver bad news. Families could tell just from the muted body language and the somber expressions on their faces what was in store. Over the last twenty-four hours of waiting, the regular updates for the families of the trapped miners had developed into a ritual all of its own. Like a White House press briefing, every word was analyzed, every inflexion given weight and import. Some family members wrote down Weir's words, taking especial note when he mentioned anything involving time; when the drill was due to arrive, what time it was due to start drilling, and so on. For time brought hope, and with hope came the possibility of an end to the nightmare.

As the time approached for, say, the drill to arrive, everyone would start to look at their watches, glancing at the door expectantly, watching anxiously for the familiar figure of Weir in his blue jeans and T-shirt. When he arrived in his red pick-up a cry of: 'Update, update' would ring out, and those in the parking lot or in the backyard would come running, rapidly swelling the hall to capacity, people straining to hear what he had to say, watching carefully for the manner in which he said it. 'You could hear a pin drop,' recalled one family member.

For some, however, it was too much to bear. They stayed outside and let others listen to Weir speak. 'Only tell us if it's good news,' they would say. So much hope, so much dependence invested in a few hastily chosen sentences. Such a burden of anxiety placed on those words.

Such a weight placed on John Weir's shoulders, too. This was not his normal terrain. He was more used to discussing drainage, infill, and reclamation, inhabiting a world of excavators, rigs and pumps. Machines didn't burst into tears or answer back; nor for the most part did the miners with whom he dealt from day to day. He had been the company's spokesman when the hijacked Flight 93 had crashed on PBS land at Shanksville, but nothing had prepared him for this, standing before a roomful of people, seeing the hope in their eyes, the anticipation in their faces.

With so much rumor and conjecture swirling around, not just in the media but in the community at large, the Governor had told the families not to believe anything they saw or heard on TV or the radio. For good or ill, they would get the correct information first from official sources via John Weir, and without any sugar coating. As a result, the TV in the fire hall was watched little, and then mainly towards the end of the rescue. As MSHA spokeswoman Amy Louviere noted, 'We are very sensitive to the fact that in any mine accident the families must hear the news first. Sadly, accidents don't always have a positive outcome.'

In the first few hours of the rescue the families were given news as and when there was any to release. All that changed after the Governor met with them. He took John Weir aside and, looking him firmly in the eye, requested that he update the families every hour – as the families themselves wanted. When Weir told him that it took him at least an hour and twenty minutes to visit the rescue site and the mine, get a fix on progress and then drive back to the fire hall, the Governor was firm. 'John, on the hour, every hour.' 'Thank God for the Pennsylvania State Police – and I knew most of them – thank God for all the guys who knew that I was trying to make that trip in an hour,' John Weir said later, remembering his hair-raising round-trips.

At 3.00 on Friday morning, 26 July, he would rather have been anywhere else on earth than walking into Sipesville fire hall. The previous evening the Governor had predicted that the drill would break through between three and four in the morning. The families in the hall clung to those words, ready and waiting in the early hours of Friday to be given the news that they craved.

Shortly before Weir was due to drive to the fire hall, however, all hell had broken loose at the rescue site. Federal and state officials who were trying to grab a couple of hours' sleep in their cars were roughly awakened and told that, at a little before two o'clock, the drill in the rescue shaft had broken at a depth of 105 feet. Engineers were checking and rechecking the machinery, but the situation did not look good. No one knew for sure how long it would take to retrieve the 1,500-pound steel carbide drill bit. It might take a couple of hours, it might take a week. It was John Weir's job to break the news to the families.

As soon as he walked into the room they knew it was bad news. They could tell just from the way he walked. While he spoke about the broken drill there was silence, then mayhem, people shouting, cursing and crying. Some walked out and just drove off into the night, others ran into the backyard, where they broke down and wept. Sandy Popernack got into her pick-up, drove to the rescue site and refused to leave. Amid the commotion in the fire hall, one voice rang out, that of Tonya Mayhugh, Blaine's sister-in-law. 'Have you heard any more tapping?' she shouted. The room suddenly stilled. Weir, dropping his head to hide from them the tears rolling down his cheeks, spoke the one word they all dreaded: 'No'. In a matter of moments the room virtually emptied as people spilled out into the night air, their frustration and fear almost palpable. 'That was the lowest point,' recalls the Reverend Joseph Beer, who had been at Sipesville with the families from the start. Like most of the others in that room, Robert Pugh's girlfriend Cindy Thomas now feared the worst. 'We thought that they weren't going to survive,' she admits. This was a downdate with a vengeance.

Outside, families gathered around the picnic tables in the backyard. Everyone was exhausted, weary of the emotional burden they had been carrying for what seemed like an eternity. 'I just don't know what to think any more,' someone said in the darkness, as family members, friends and supporters tried to absorb the distressing news. 'Well, I do,' responded Margie Mayhugh. 'I'm Blaine's mother and I know what to think. They are dead. I know they are dead.'

Then she bowed her head and burst into tears, sobs racking her body. Karen Schafer, not only a friend of Leslie Mayhugh's, but also of the family, went over to hug her and for the next few minutes Margie took out her frustration by hitting Karen's back and shoulders. Blaine's mother was not the only one sobbing that night. As Rona Hemminger, a close friend of Sue Ellen Unger, remembers, 'That was the time we all cried. At that point we feared that it was all over and that the next news would be that they were all dead.'

At this bleak moment Tasha Stewart, a speech therapist who works with Leslie Mayhugh at the Beverly nursing home, suggested that they gather round in a circle and pray for God's guidance. As Tasha led the Foy and Mayhugh families in early-morning prayer, it was clear that Leslie Mayhugh was on the point of collapse. It was only by the efforts of her friend Karen Schafer and her sister Amy, who stood on either side of her holding her hands, that she managed to remain standing. They prayed for guidance, strength and the safe return of their loved ones. Afterwards, everyone felt a sense of peace.

'I feel good and clear-headed now,' Leslie told Karen some time later, linking arms with her and walking her away from the others. When they had reached a quiet patch of ground, Leslie said that she wanted to tell her friend how the funeral of her husband and father should be arranged if the worst happened. She knew, she said, that when she was told the news she would not be able to cope. 'They worked together, they died together and I want them buried together,' she continued, going on to ask Karen to make sure that her husband and father were viewed together in their coffins at the same funeral home and buried side by side in the graveyard at Beechdale Brethren church in Berlin. Remarkably, at almost the same time, Denise Foy, Tom's wife, was having a similar conversation with Kathy Engle, during which she expressed the same sentiments and requested the same funeral arrangements. Neither mother nor daughter had discussed the matter with each other beforehand.

Equally uncanny was the bond that existed between those above ground and those trapped below. As family members chatted among themselves the conversation invariably returned to what their men might be talking about. They knew that they would be discussing hunting trips and fishing expeditions both past, and future and wondering how their families were bearing up. Of course, they knew that they would be praying – everyone was. Later, these assumptions were found to have been, in the main, unerringly accurate. On one occasion Leslie Mayhugh guessed, half in jest, that her father, Tucker Foy, a renowned trencherman, would probably be sizing up which of his fellow miners to eat first. Sure enough, when he emerged from the black pit, he confessed that the thought had crossed his mind. He wouldn't say whom he had selected, though – or how serious he was.

*

Tom Foy had good reason to feel hungry. The men below ground had not eaten since Thursday afternoon, when Tom Foy and Ron Hileman, scouting around the section, had found Dennis Hall's lunch pail floating on the flood water, its lid still in place. The corned beef sandwich made by Hall's wife Paulette had stayed dry, though it was rather stale. It was passed round and everyone took a bite. Everyone except Blaine Mayhugh, that is, who snorted that it wasn't even enough to get him started, and John Unger, who was too wound up to eat. They washed it down with a bottle of Mountain Dew and another of Pepsi that Paulette Hall had also packed. Hearing about the sandwich, talk-show host David Letterman would later quip, 'It ain't exactly the all-you-can-eat buffet.' From then on, apart from three gallons of distilled water, used to top up machine batteries and a couple more fizzy drinks that Foy found on a waterlogged machine, the only nourishment they got was from their fevered imaginations. They discussed their favorite food – most opted for steaks – while Robert Pugh lovingly told them about a plump 18-pound wild turkey he had shot and eaten earlier that year. When Mark Popernack asked them what they wanted most – beer, snuff or hot chocolate – most of the shivering crew chose the hot drink.

By now the water seemed to be gradually receding, and apart from the fact that they were trapped, the cold and damp were now their greatest threats. Every man was shivering with cold, every man was wet, and all of them were aware of the potentially fatal effects of hypothermia. They took off their shoes and wrung out their socks, wrapped themselves in the thick, damp ventilation canvas to protect themselves from the worst of the chill from the mine floor, and huddled together tepee-style to keep warm – except that none of them ever felt warm. 'Things were getting pretty weak,' recalled Robert Pugh who, with the other miners, was becoming increasingly concerned about the health of their crew chief, Randy Fogle. Characteristically, Fogle dismissed his coughing and chest pains as heartburn caused by the oily fumes from the compressed air. The others were not so sure.

What they did know was that, above everything else, they wanted to be out of this blackness. 'It seemed like it was taking so much time to find us,' Pugh said later. 'Time was something we didn't have.' As the minutes since the drill fell silent ticked by into hours, the doubts began to crowd in. All the while they prayed – for themselves, for their families, and for the nine other miners who they were certain had died in the first fury of the flood. 'I've never prayed so much in my life,' Robert Pugh told his local Catholic journal afterwards. 'God is the one who got us through this. We all knew we had to rely on God. Faith in God is all that mattered.'

By late Friday morning the weak jokes about the guys above knocking off for the night no longer raised even the glimmer of a smile. They feared that the rescuers had decided to move the drill to another site, or that they had assumed that they were dead because they had not heard any tapping for twelve hours. 'We thought they had broke down or given up on us,' Blaine Mayhugh admitted. Yet, when one gave in to doubts about their chances of survival, the others would rally to pull him through. A touch of dark sarcasm usually worked, one or other of them joking about whether they would be paid overtime for the days they were trapped and idle underground. 'We worked together and when one would get down, the others would pick him up,' Mayhugh added. 'I got through because of those men.'

Others, besides God and the friends trapped with them, were doing all they could to help them get through the ordeal. In fact, their rescuers 240 feet above them had not stopped work for the night – they had gone fishing. They were trying to land the biggest catch of their lives, a massive 1,500 pounder. In the early hours they lowered a camera down the rescue shaft to see what the problem was, but the 30-inch drill bit, which had broken 105 feet down into the earth, proved to be an elusive catch when they lowered grabs to try to snag it. The Yost drillers would hook the drill but then, like a wily trout, it would break free while they were teasing and easing it to the surface, falling back to the foot of the shaft. On one occasion they brought it to within a few feet of the lip of the hole, only for it to slip away again. It was beyond frustrating, especially for the Yost crew, who are known as the best in the business. A rival driller who had once lost a similar bit said at the time, 'We dropped down and hit our bit on the first shock and in fifteen minutes our bit was to the top of the hole and dogged off, ready to be removed.' Roughly translated, it had taken them just fifteen minutes to retrieve their broken drill bit on that occasion. Far from gloating, he was voicing his amazement at how fate seemed to conspire against the highly admired crew.

After several hours of fruitless fishing, it was decided to bring in a second drill crew and prepare the site for another rescue shaft. While the ground was being prepared for the crew from Falcon Drilling in Indiana, orders went out from the command center to find a special hook with which to capture the elusive bit. Rescue workers contacted a specialist engineer, Frank Stockdale, who manages a tool-shop works in Jefferson County with ninety-five employees. Stockdale said that he could make the required tool, but warned that, under normal circumstances, it would take three or four days to machine. These circumstances were not normal, however. With the Governor, the rescue teams, indeed the whole of America and beyond, now focused on the rescue, he and his men broke all records. The hook was ready in just three hours. 'When they call you up and tell you a National Guard helicopter will be waiting to pick it up when you're done, you get a sense of urgency,' Stockdale remarked dryly.

In the first few hours after the drill broke, however, millions of Americans slept through the night, oblivious of the dramatic setback. Although a reporter for a local TV news station, Bob Allen, went on air at 6.30 to say that there seemed to be some difficulty with the rescue drill, it was not until Governor Schweiker appeared on the morning *Today* show that the wider world discovered that the rescue efforts had stalled. By now more than 200 correspondents and cameramen from every national TV station and newspaper group, as well as journalists from abroad, were camped at the media center at the disused Giant Eagle supermarket.

The story had struck a universal nerve. Not only did the drama expose our deep-seated horror of being buried alive, but also our instinctive faith in, and optimism about, the resilience of the human spirit and the resourcefulness of the human mind. These were beliefs that had been severely dented, particularly in America, following the 9/11 atrocity and a number of subsequent corporate scandals, notably the collapse of the Enron power company. Indeed, several cartoons published in papers at the time of the rescue suggested plugging the mine hole with disgraced chief executive officers.

Messages of hope, prayers and good wishes poured into Somerset, not just from neighboring states but from as far afield as Tasmania, Scotland and Japan, while the Sipesville fire station website was inundated with good-luck e-mails. It seemed that everyone in Somerset County was being seen as a hero or heroine of the rescue attempt. When Andrea Policicchio was photographed by a local newspaper cameraman looking out from the window of the cafeteria she owns in Boswell, a 'Nine for Nine' sign above her head, she was amazed to receive a deluge of mail from strangers, including a request for an autographed photo. One admirer, a buggy-tour operator, even offered her a free buggy ride.

The intense interest ensured that competition among the media to be first with the news was fierce and frenetic, and when the veteran tabloid-TV journalist Geraldo Rivera arrived in Somerset the pace quickened further. The local community, however, proved to be equally adept at protecting their own against what they considered to be media intrusion. When Rivera and his TV crew tried to set up outside the home of Bill Arnold's elderly parents on his farm, they found themselves escorted off the land under the watchful eyes of local state troopers. Local clergy became the equivalent of nightclub doormen, preventing journalists from infiltrating the fire hall where the families were gathered, and throwing out the odd one who managed to slip through this ecclesiastical net. While their language was not always, perhaps, what they would have used from the pulpit, their brisk assertiveness ensured that the families, already burdened, were not bothered by inquisitive strangers. Photographers who tried to get on to the rescue site were ejected with rather more vigor – and rather less argument – by Navy SEALs.

For the men and women working at the rescue site and in the command center at the mine, the media whirlwind literally passed them by. Their only focus was on the men below ground. Nothing else mattered. Bill Arnold witnessed this adrenalin-fueled commitment that Friday morning as the engineers were setting up the second drill site, a few yards from the stalled rescue shaft. In their haste to retrieve the dislodged drill bit, workers had discarded an 8oo-pound drill steel on the site where the second shaft was to be drilled. It needed to be moved.

At that moment a team of six miners, their faces and hands still jet black from working at the mine site setting pumps, appeared on the site. 'What do you need?' asked one. Arnold explained the problem. Without more ado except for a cry of 'Let's get it done,' the men grabbed the drill steel as though it were a toothpick, hoisted it on to their shoulders and moved it out of the way. No arguments, no time-wasting. 'Let's get it done' became, for Arnold, a phrase that defined the team spirit among the rescue workers. As he says, 'It was so humbling to see these guys working so hard and diligently to save their buddies underground. They were just frustrated by the delay.' At the mine itself, owner Dave Rebuck had summoned the nine miners who had escaped the flood and told them to take the day off. There wasn't even a discussion. Next day, all nine were back at the mine, hauling and setting pipes for the pumps. This was no longer a job, this was personal. In truth, too, they wanted to be with their work brothers. Only other miners understood just what they had been through. It was especially hard for Joe Kostyk, whose ten-year-old daughter Stacey had pleaded with him not to go back to the mine. Gently he explained to her, 'Stacey, it's like this. What if it was me in that hole? Wouldn't you want their dads to come back and get me?'

Even though the second drill started grinding into the earth at 1.15 on Friday afternoon, the miners were a frustrated and concerned band of brothers, anxious about the delay in reaching their buddies. Doctors called in to brief the command team at the mine were increasingly worried that after more than thirty hours below ground, the miners would be suffering from the effects of hypothermia. Mine officials were warned that when a body is immersed in water the skin and tissues cool quickly, which in turn leads to an overall drop in body temperature. When the body temperature falls from the normal 98.6 degrees Fahrenheit to below 90 degrees serious complications set in. At 86 degrees a person may become unconscious, and may die if his or her temperature falls any lower. As a result, the sense of urgency among the rescue teams was dramatically heightened, especially as nothing had been heard from the trapped men since Thursday morning. 'The doctors were warning us that with every passing hour the men's condition would be worsening, but it was frustrating because we couldn't get the drill bit out,' Kevin Stricklin remembers.

Not all the news was bad. The arrival of the two diesel pumps at the mine, together with the successful drilling of more boreholes into the mine, had made an enormous difference to the amount of water being pumped out of the workings, and the level inside the mine was subsiding. Even so, charts and soundings showed that the water level was still higher than the miners' heads, leading rescuers to assume that only the air bubble was keeping the tide of water at bay.

By mid-morning on Friday, with preparations for the second drill hole well under way, the rescuers decided to use seismic equipment to see if there were any signs of life below ground. The problem was that they could not turn off the compressor that provided the vital flow of air. Everything else was shut down, including traffic, with state troopers stopping cars and trucks driving by the site on Highway 985 at 10.30 so that they would not interfere with readings taken by the sensitive equipment. The seismic test proved inconclusive, however, the noise and vibration of the compressor contaminating all readings, effectively masking any signals from below ground. At the same time, doctors at the site warned that the effects of cold on the men might have made them sluggish and weak, so that they would not even have the strength to hammer on the pipe. The ambiguous news did little to raise morale among the waiting families.

A couple of hours later, engineers tested the theory that the nine men might have broken into the disused Saxman mine to escape from the water. By 1.30 in the afternoon – just 15 minutes after the second drill started up – a new 6-inch borehole into the Saxman mine was completed. There was no response when the rescue workers tapped on the drill steel, so Bob 'Mr Microphone' Zaremski, a specialist in listening technology who had been brought from Akron, Ohio, was asked to lower his state-of-the-art probe, camera and transmitter down the hole. All the camera showed was water in the mine gallery.

The probe was left in the shaft and every five minutes or so Zaremski would call out his standard message in the hope that the miners would respond. 'Stay where you are. Tap ten times and seismic will pick you up.' For the next eight hours while he endlessly repeated his mantra all he heard in response was dripping or running water. 'What we were hoping for was the water level would recede enough so that some air would cross through, so a voice could resonate and come across the void,' he explains.

With no signal from the miners for more than twenty-four hours, and with doctors at the site offering a gloomy forecast as to their possible condition even if they were still alive, things were looking increasingly serious. It would still be many hours before the second rescue shaft was completed. Everyone was now planning for a 'best worst-case' scenario, namely that the miners were alive, but unconscious or injured.

In a sense, Danny Sacco of the Special Medical Response Team had been waiting for this moment all his life. With his friendly manner and fashionable glasses and clothes, he looks more like a store manager than a rescue expert and paramedic. Yet in September 2001 he had been at the site of the Twin Towers in Manhattan twelve hours after they collapsed, and spent nine depressing days searching through the ruins and rubble for survivors. When he and his colleagues from SMRT arrived at Quecreek he was determined that this time it was going to be different, not just because he felt that he owed it to the memory of his father, Ross, who was killed in a mining accident when Danny was just six, but also because here there was a genuine, if slim, chance of a successful outcome.

As the drillers on the second rig drove the bit into the ground, Sacco and his team were brainstorming the different medical and logistical problems involved in bringing the miners out alive and then safely transporting them to hospital. Fetching them to the surface was not as simple as it seemed. Even after the drill had broken through and the yellow rescue capsule been deployed, the trapped miners would have to be manhandled into the metal cage. If, as was now expected, they were injured or unconscious, it would be extremely difficult in such a confined space for a rescuer, himself sent down in the cage, to haul an injured man into what was little more than a small box.

In addition, even if they managed that, the miner would have to be hauled to the surface on his own. If he was unconscious, or lost consciousness on the journey to the surface, his head and neck would drop, constricting his windpipe to such an extent that he would choke to death. For this reason, SMRT needed urgently to devise a method that would enable a rescuer to get a miner into the capsule in a safe and effective way and get him to the surface alive. 'From the very beginning we were planning the worst-case scenario where we had to bring nine guys who were alive but injured and unconscious to the surface,' Danny Sacco explains.

They looked at every possibility. Since the rescue cage had never been used in an emergency before there were discussions about using a cable and harness instead. This idea was discounted because if an unconscious miner became trapped against the unlined sides of the shaft on the way up, he might easily lose a limb as the winch continued to pull him to the surface. Even so, they tested the yellow rescue cage to make sure that it could do the job. One of the rescue workers, Sam Brunatti, who weighs in at between 330 and 350 pounds – no one knows for sure because household scales won't hold him – was chosen as the guinea pig. The 6-foot-3-inch heavyweight was suspended from a crane inside the capsule to reassure the rescue team that it would carry even the heaviest of the trapped miners. Later the Governor tested it, just to be sure.

Working with what kit they had in their emergency trucks, the SMRT people had to devise a low-level pulley system that could enable a rescuer to ratchet a heavy, possibly unconscious miner into the upright capsule while ensuring that his neck and back were fully supported. After much discussion Shawn Houck, an SMRT rescue specialist, suggested using a hand-operated 'come-along', a device that would provide the necessary leverage to lift a man into the capsule, as well as modifying an upper-body stretcher – a stiffened wraparound jacket, not unlike a straitjacket, that supports the injured person's head, neck and back – so that when the miner was hauled to the surface his neck and head remained upright. The first prototypes did not work effectively but, by a process of trial and error they managed to adapt an upper-body stretcher that would do the job.

The next task was to train the rescue team – the men who would be sent down to bring the miners out – to operate the come-along and modified stretcher in the dark, confined conditions that they would experience in the mine. Fortunately the mine-rescue team from Enlow Fork, near Pittsburgh, currently the American mine-rescue champions, had been deployed to Quecreek to help in the rescue. They spent hours with the SMRT personnel in one of Bill Arnold's barns, training to use the ingenious rescue devices. Just as ingenious, but rather easier to operate, was a credit-card-size monitor previously devised by Dr Richard Kunkle. One of these would be placed on each miner's chest to monitor and record heart rhythms and other functions. The tiny monitors could be easily brought to the surface, and transferred to a computer, allowing doctors to assess whether trained medics should go down the shaft to treat any injuries or any other medical problems.

Even when a miner reached the surface he would still be at risk. After discussions with the Navy SEALs, Sacco and his colleagues realized that if a miner covered in coal dust were to be placed straight into a decompression chamber in which the atmosphere was highly oxygenated, there was a strong probability of an explosion, because of the danger of spontaneous combustion inherent in coal dust. In the light of this, they brought

Ed Hutchinson (*foreground*), chief of the Greensburg Volunteer Fire Department, catches a nap among weary rescue workers during a break from drilling operations at the rescue site, 27 July

Below: Surrounded by rescue workers, Dr Richard Kunkle of the Special Medical Response Team (*in headset*) talks to one of the trapped miners after a microphone was lowered to them and communication was at last established, 27 July

Above: Rescue workers rest as they watch the air lock being placed on shaft No. 1, 27 July

Right: Exhaustion, but also determination, shows on one of the rescuers' faces

Below: Even at night, anxious onlookers, some of them relations of the trapped men, waited and watched. Inset: The shrine to the trapped miners that Father Breski established in a local Catholic church; the figurines were lent by Robert Pugh's father

Above: The rescue cage is lowered into position. The tension among some of the onlookers is almost palpable

Below: A few minutes later, the cage begins its long journey to the cavern where the trapped miners wait

Above: Rescue workers applaud as a miner is brought to the surface

Below: First man up – Randy Fogle reaches the surface at 1.00 a.m. on Sunday, 28 July

Top: Triumph – Doug Custer, one of the miners who escaped, hugs fellow miner Larry Summerville in celebration

Right: Bill and Lori Arnold, on whose farm the rescue was carried out

Below: Last man out – flanked by state troopers, the Governor (*center right, in blue shirt*) helps with the stretcher carrying Mark Popernack

Above: Rescued miner Blaine Mayhugh relieved to be home with his wife, Leslie, and children Kelsey (*left*) and Tyler. He vows never to go underground again

Below: Local children celebrate when President Bush visits Pittsburgh to honor the rescued and the rescuers. The youngsters had their sign autographed by the rescued miners

Above, left: A tearful Diana Schad, wife of Ron Schad, tells the author about the harrowing ordeal her husband and his coworkers went through as they scrambled to escape the flood

Above, right: Ebullient as ever, Tom Foy hugs a family friend after a service of thanksgiving at the Casebeer Lutheran Church, just yards from the rescue site

Below: John Unger greets the President, watched by (*from left*) Blaine Mayhugh, Ron Hileman, John Phillippi and Robert Pugh. The President said the rescue symbolized 'the spirit of America'

Above: From shops to private homes and fast-food outlets, Somerset County expressed its belief in, and gratitude for, a miracle. Families of the trapped miners stayed at the Sipesville fire hall (*main photo*) during their long vigil as they anxiously awaited news of their loved ones

Below: Somerset County Fair, 18 August — and the miners provide the main attraction

in another agency, the Hazardous Materials Response Team (HAZMAT), to set up a decontamination unit in a tent next to the decompression chambers. While a doctor quickly checked a rescued miner's vital signs, HAZMAT would cut off the man's clothes and wash him before he was placed in the chamber. As they had learned from the Navy divers, all this had to be done in just fifteen minutes, before the rescued man began to suffer the effects of decompression sickness, with potentially fatal results.

The next issue was how to transfer the miner from the capsule to the decontamination tent quickly and safely. Doctors on site warned that if the men were suffering from severe hypothermia, which was likely, then any jostling or shaking might cause a potentially fatal heart dysfunction. There followed a discussion about whether to carry the men in a Stokes litter, a large deep stretcher of wire mesh on a tubular metal framework, or in a motorized cart. The rescue coordinators in the command center favored a vehicle, while the SMRT boys preferred the stretcher. In the end, Sacco insisted that man-handling was the smoothest and safest way to carry the miners from the rescue shaft to the decontamination site. To make sure, three teams of stretcher bearers, comprising of local firemen and SMRT members, spent hours carefully rehearsing every single move from getting the miner out of the capsule to walking smoothly to the medical area, even using volunteers of similar weight and height to the trapped miners as guinea-pig stretcher cases.

With the miners, theoretically, now safely at the field medical site, and with any injuries stabilized by doctors and the men decompressed in the chambers, the next problem was to get them to hospital quickly. Sacco arranged with the National Guard for nine helicopters to be on stand-by although, with the weather forecasters predicting storms, nine life-support ambulances were also placed on notice. Sacco and his colleagues were determined to plan for all eventualities.

Now the medical preparations began to involve the miners' families. During a visit to the rescue site to see for themselves the progress of the second drill, wives and partners were told that they had a vital role to play. Officers from the Navy SEAL team carefully explained that when their men were brought to the surface, they might be unconscious or confused. They might even seem lifeless due to the effects of hypothermia. 'A cold body is not a dead body,' the women were assured. They were also told that they would be needed at the medical site to calm and encourage their disoriented partners as they were placed inside the narrow and confining decompression chambers. Then doctors questioned them about any medical conditions or allergies among the rescued men that the medical staff needed to look out for. 'In a strange way it really lifted their spirits,' recalled Cathy Custer, who was now quartered with the families at Sipesville. 'They felt that they were able to do something positive, that their husbands had been made real flesh-and-blood people again.'

Some time later, however, they were suddenly informed that they would no longer be required at the site when the men were lifted out. Only vital mining and medical personnel would be allowed to be present. It was a bitter blow on a day of despair, disappointment and delay. The continuing uncertainty jangled nerves and frayed tempers. Everyone was on tenterhooks. Several wives of the trapped miners burst into tears when a representative from Black Wolf arrived at the fire hall on Friday with the men's paychecks, which he proceeded to hand out. For the women involved, the gesture signified a kind of finality. In a last ironic twist, to the men's pay of around $1,000 had been added a safety bonus, since there had been no safety violations in the mine during the previous few weeks.

The accumulated frustration and anxiety boiled over when John Weir brought Dave Rebuck to the fire hall to talk to the families. Outside a thunderstorm was brewing, and inside

Rebuck was deluged with complaints. An angry Blaine Mayhugh Sr fiercely attacked him over the delays, adding his belief that everyone was, in his words, 'blowing smoke up their asses'. He became so vociferous in denouncing a clearly shocked Rebuck that others in the hall shouted at him to calm down. Even though Mayhugh later apologized to the mine owner for his outburst, he continued his loud grumbling when the Governor arrived to brief the families. Like many others, he was most irritated by the continually changing timeframe, which at once raised expectations and then dashed them when drilling targets weren't met because of unforeseen events, as when the drill struck bands of hard rock. The discussion between the two men continued at the front of the hall after the main meeting had ended. Mayhugh's daughter-in-law, Leslie, noticed a black smudge of coal dust on the Governor's cheek. 'Don't tell me he gave you a black eye,' she joked, neatly defusing the confrontation. In a curious way, her remark and her father's criticisms led to the Governor's being accepted by the families, who by now had become a close-knit community. After that he would always greet Blaine Mayhugh Sr by name, and from then on people seemed to see him as one of their own.

On Friday afternoon, US Department of Labor assistant secretary, Dave Lauriski, arrived on site to take overall command of the rescue operation. He recognized at once the frustration on the ground but, from long experience, knew that it was vital that the men in charge should not allow emotion to cloud their judgment, or despair to weaken their efforts. They had a plan, and they had to stick to it. 'We had got to a point in the mission where people get nervous,' he recalled. 'I wanted to make sure that we kept focus and stuck to our decisions.'

A third-generation miner – 'I'm a coal miner and damn proud of it' – until he went into mine safety, Lauriski had been involved over the years in numerous life-and-death mine rescues. He had first come to prominence in 1984 for the way he directed a dangerous rescue operation at the Wilberg mine in Utah, where a fire claimed the lives of twenty-seven miners. That and other experiences had taught him that control was the key to success. In the light of this, he immediately ordered that the command center, then based at the mine, should be moved a mile up the road to the drill site, where there was so much concentrated activity that an atmosphere of organized chaos prevailed. 'The road to the drill site was like rush hour in Washington,' Lauriski recalls. 'The state police were literally besides themselves.' The media, friends and relations of the miners and curious sightseers were clogging both the roads and the site, which was enveloped by a cloud of sandy dust thrown up by the drilling and the heavy trucks and machinery. Yet the key players in the rescue now needed to maintain their composure and remove all other distractions for the next vital few hours of the recovery operation. Lauriski, however, took this in his stride. Nor was he as concerned as some of his colleagues about the health of the trapped miners. Previous experience – notably the successful rescue of Josh Dennis, a ten-year-old Boy Scout who went missing in a Utah silver mine for five days in 1989 – had taught him that people, especially miners, can survive for long periods underground.

He radiated that sense of confidence when he and the Governor visited the families later that afternoon. With good news in such short supply, the announcement that the elusive drill bit in the first rescue hole had at last been retrieved after fourteen painstaking hours was cause for cheering. A replacement had been flown in by National Guard helicopter. None the less, the mood of sober reflection quickly returned, the Governor leading the families in prayer, and reading a passage from Psalm 46: 'God is our refuge and strength, always ready to help in times of trouble.'

Afterwards the Unger family approached Assistant Secretary Lauriski and asked if he would call Mary Unger, the mother of

John Unger. Aged eighty-seven and unable to travel from her home, she was growing increasingly anxious about the progress of the rescue attempts. 'It's awful, the waiting,' she told reporters who called on her. 'It seems like things just keep going wrong.' Lauriski did indeed call her to tell her of the rescue's progress, his call doing much to ease her concerns.

He could not entirely assuage her doubts, though, nor those of the other family members. No earthly agency could. When Father Barry Baroni arrived at the fire hall from Johnstown that evening to offer spiritual support to Dennis Hall's wife Paulette and her two sons, Justin and Derek, he couldn't help but feel that overpowering sense of doubt and anxiety. 'The families were numb with fatigue,' he said later. 'You could see the lack of sleep in their eyes. You could feel the worry and concern. Yet if there was a lack of hope among them, no one expressed it. Instead, everyone made an effort to express how grateful they were for the marvelous support they were receiving.'

That night the families, friends and supporters of the trapped miners held a candlelit prayer vigil inside the fire hall. Similar services were held through the county and the country; a service in the Roman Catholic church at nearby Acosta featured a tableau – almost a shrine – decorated with nine figurines of miners lent by Robert Pugh's father, as well as nine symbolic candles and nine miners' helmets.

At the fire hall, there was also a display of nine miners' helmets and nine candles, with one larger candle to represent God. Ironically, one of the helmets, chosen at random from the lamp room at Quecreek mine, was that of Doug Custer, who had escaped the flood. During the service the congregation sang hymns and listened to readings from the Bible. Then, as the name of each missing miner was called out, a member of his family lit a candle by a helmet. Some offered up sentence prayers, other simply held hands in a giant circle. It was a moving occasion, prompting Father Jack O'Malley to remark, 'I was impressed by the strength of faith and the positive mental attitude of people.'

As the ten candles glowed in the evening light, a message of support from the families of those killed aboard the hijacked United Flight 93, which had been received via e-mail, was read out. It said: 'During our time of tragedy, you extended yourselves to us and tirelessly continued to do so. We consider you our family, and we sincerely hope and pray that the recovery effort will be successful in bringing your loved ones home.' Governor Schweiker welcomed the message, saying that it symbolized the way the nation had responded to the trapped miners.

Like everyone else who was there, the Governor was emotionally consumed by the drama. At a news conference in front of what had once been the Pennsylvania Lottery sales counter at the Giant Eagle supermarket, he had tears in his eyes when he pledged to journalists, 'We are doing everything mechanically, humanly, intellectually and technologically we can.'

Back at the rescue both drills were working that night– by around ten o'clock the second drill was down 48 feet – and the water inside the mine was subsiding rapidly, at a rate of around a foot every hour. Amid the atmosphere of quiet contemplation and subdued conversation inside the fire hall, John Unger's young nephew, Riley, was in party mood. The eight-year-old was cheerfully organizing the homecoming celebration for Uncle John. After he asked family members what food they were going to bring to the party, he wondered aloud about what to write on the celebration cake. They chose the words of Unger's favorite song, 'Don't Worry Be Happy'. At that moment everyone thought of his big, beaming face. And they knew he would be at the party.

Chapter VII

'WHAT TOOK YOU GUYS SO LONG?'

IT IS A TRADITION almost as old as Pennsylvania itself. Every year on 2 February, thousands of people descend on the pleasant town of Punxsutawney, about seventy miles north of Quecreek, for the annual Groundhog Day ceremony, in which the local groundhog, Punxsutawney Phil, makes his prediction as to the length of the winter. If he sees his shadow when he emerges from his burrow, then there will be six more weeks of winter weather; no shadow foretells an early spring. This annual event was made internationally famous after a 1993 Hollywood movie that starred Bill Murray as a cynical TV reporter who finds himself the victim of a terrible fate, doomed to relive endlessly the events of Groundhog Day.

On Saturday, 27 July 2002, it seemed that Groundhog Day had come south to Quecreek. In the early hours of that morning MSHA engineer Gerry Davis had been manning the fort, overseeing drilling from the command center at the mine while the other rescue coordinators snatched a couple of hours of much needed rest. Everything was going well. The water was being pumped out at an appreciable rate, and the two drills were working in tandem, driving down towards the trapped men. So Davis was scarcely able to believe it when he was told that the drill in the first rescue shaft had broken down at virtually the same time and the same place as on the previous evening.

The problem was that the replacement 30-inch bit was in fact about a half-inch larger in diameter than the one that broke off at 105 feet. While this sort of discrepancy is not uncommon among drill bits of nominally identical dimensions, it meant that when the Yost drill team had started drilling again the new, slightly larger drill bit had had to chew rock and earth all the way down to the level at which the first bit had broken. By the time it reached the point at which drilling had been forced to stop on the previous day, the drill was worn out. For an hour it had been spinning on its shaft and only gone down 9 inches. Just to make life interesting, the second drill, which had reached 103 feet – still nearly 140 feet from the miners – was reported to be out of commission soon afterwards. A worn shock absorber meant that, for the time being, it was silent while the defective part was replaced. Meanwhile, one of the main borehole pumps sucking water out of the Mains section was being repaired. Rescue workers observed that Murphy's Law, which states that anything that can go wrong, will go wrong, seemed to be in the ascendant that night.

As a result, at three o'clock in the morning, Gerry Davis found himself going shopping. Not surprisingly, 30-inch drill bits are in short supply at that time of day. He consulted Dave Rebuck, who told him, after making his own inquiries, that the nearest place from which they could obtain a replacement bit was in Cleveland, Ohio, more than 150 miles away. Once more valuable hours would be wasted in transporting the drill bit to the rescue site, hours that they simply didn't have. Rebuck did know someone with a 26-inch drill bit, which was available down the road in nearby Somerset. Davis sucked in his breath. The rescue capsule was 22 inches wide, which meant that using it in a 26-inch-diameter shaft would be a tight squeeze. A very tight squeeze – just 2 inches to spare all round between the capsule and the shaft walls. A single dislodged rock in the shaft, which, when completed, would be the length of a football field, could spell disaster.

The MSHA engineer consulted the man now in command of the rescue operation, Dave Lauriski. He could scarcely believe what Davis was telling him. For most of that evening he had been emphasizing to engineers, drillers and anyone else who would listen that his gravest concern was no longer the water or the drilling, but the dangers of operating an untried rescue capsule in an unlined shaft. His main fear was that the shaft would collapse on the capsule as it was bringing a miner to the surface. At the very least a rockfall could block its progress and they already knew that water was a hazard in the shaft itself. At a depth of 70 feet they had hit an underground stream, and they feared that the force of the gushing water would dislodge loose rocks below. Rescuers realized that for a miner, already weakened by three days underground without food and in terrible conditions, to be trapped, perhaps for hours, beneath what was effectively an ice-cold shower would severely reduce his chances of survival.

In the early hours of Saturday morning Davis and Lauriski debated whether to wait either for the second shaft to be completed, or for a replacement 30-inch bit, or whether to go with the smaller replacement drill bit. It was a tough decision, but in the end they felt that as the rescue capsule was rounded at the bottom it could just squeeze past the lip that would be formed where the 30-inch hole shrank to 26 inches. They decided to gamble. By 4.30 in the morning the new drill was at the site and had to been fitted to the rig, ready for action.

The revised drilling operation brought into sharp relief the contingency plans being formulated to rescue a miner should he become trapped inside the metal capsule within the escape tunnel. Much depended on the second shaft, which would be used by the rescue team stationed on the surface to come to the aid of the trapped man and the other miners. They decided to rig a video camera to the base of the untried rescue capsule so that they would have a bird's-eye view of its progress down the shaft, and perhaps be able to identify any problem areas and take steps to deal with them. At the same time, they also ensured that the capsule, fitted with an escape hatch at the bottom, was equipped with pulleys and enough rope and rigging to allow the miner trapped inside to be hauled back down by rescuers. Finally, they also calculated a safe rate of ascent and descent for the capsule. Initially they decided on 30 feet a minute, then reduced that by half. In the end the rescue capsule was used at a rate of between 40 and 50 feet per minute. Above all else, however, the drilling team had to make sure that the narrower 26-inch shaft was dead straight. There was absolutely no room for error, for the slightest deviation might cause the capsule to jam in the shaft.

It was a sober meeting in the command center, newly positioned in a special MSHA trailer at the site, early on Saturday morning as Governor Schweiker was briefed on the latest developments by Dave Lauriski, his colleague from MSHA, Ray McKinney, and Richard Stickler, Director of the state's Deep Mines Safety Bureau. The good news was that, by 7.30 in the morning, the second drill was at 161 feet – only 80 feet from the trapped men – while the first drill, because of the change of bit, had only reached 130 feet. It mattered little which drill reached the men first.

The Governor was told that, however quickly the drills ground through the rock, they would, under no circumstances, break through to the trapped men until the pumps had brought the water level in the mine to 1,829 feet – about a foot below where they expected to find the miners. This was the magic figure. It was explained to Schweiker that if they broke into the chamber before the water reached that level, they risked bursting the air bubble, with the result that the flood-water would overcome the men. Much has since been made of the fact that the first drill break on Friday morning was a blessing in disguise, as it allowed the rescuers to pump out water to a safe level. In fact, the rescuers had planned from the first to bring down the water to the 1,829-foot level before allowing the drill to penetrate the chamber.

At the same time, the rescuers still had to anticipate that the men were surviving under pressure. With the water falling steadily, it seemed less likely that the men would have to be brought out under pressure using the 40-foot chamber devised by engineer Larry Neff and Dr Richard Kunkle, since the receding of the water would bring a corresponding drop in the air pressure around the miners. It was still essential, however, that the rescue shaft should somehow be 'capped off' when they broke through, to maintain the pressure in the chamber. For even though they were not going to start any rescue until the danger of drowning the men had passed, they still had to contend with a probable pressure differential between the surface and that surrounding the trapped men.

At the meeting, the Governor was told that plans were in progress to make a smaller airlock that effectively capped the drill, a task once again entrusted to Larry Neff. It was designed to be hooked up to the compressor so that, if need be, compressed air could still be piped down to the men. It would also be equipped with a pressure valve that would allow rescue workers to gradually release the pressure within the mine. On advice from the Navy, they planned to bleed off the pressurized air at a rate of 0.5 psi an hour. In effect, the miners would be decompressed underground before the rescue capsule was lowered down to them.

Such, at least, was the plan, although, as the Governor by now appreciated things could – and probably would – change. Before he left to speak to the families in Sipesville, he took a handful of the limestone that had been taken from the second shaft at a depth of 150 feet. He wanted to show proof that the rescue workers were making progress. Not that he thought it would make much impression, for he knew his audience by now. The only magic number the families wanted to hear was 'Nine' followed by the word 'Alive'. They were, he sensed, 'tense, fretful but hopeful'.

'Fretful' was something of an understatement. For the men, women and children cooped up inside the Sipesville fire hall, Saturday, 27 July was sheer hell. Not only were they reliving the emotional roller-coaster of the last two days – it was now more than forty-eight hours since the trapped men had last been heard tapping – but by now conditions inside the ramshackle fire hall had become unbearable. Outside it was hot and humid – despite the fact that it was raining, temperatures hovered around 100 degrees – while inside the hall was packed with families, friends, clergy and counselors, as well as volunteers from the Red Cross, the Salvation Army and the Ladies' Auxiliary fire section. Worse still, the toilets were out of action, and the two fans in the hall proved utterly ineffective in cooling the room. Even the mining company's spokesman, John Weir, was feeling the strain, although he was heartened when the Reverend Ray Streets from the Baptist church he attended in Johnstown took the trouble to drive to the fire hall to pray with him. 'It was amazing to me,' Weir recalls. 'I'm not a religious fanatic, but those words gave me ten extra hours when I only needed eight.' For the rest of the day, he was fueled not just by caffeine and Krispy Kreme donuts, but by the power of prayer.

Others needed more earthly comforts. All through the day four doctors and a nursing team, who on Friday had set up a field medical center in the backyard, dealt with a steady stream of patients, particularly elderly relations of the miners, who had succumbed to a combination of heat, anxiety and stress. They complained of dizziness, nausea and blackouts. Some were given oxygen, others drugs to bring down their blood pressure. It was clear, though, that the best cure would be rest and recuperation, but those depended on a successful outcome to the rescue.

For Leslie Mayhugh, too, the only remedy was an end to the nightmare. She simply could not sleep. Every time she closed her eyes all she could see was water washing away her husband and her father. In her darkest moments she believed that they had been buried under the mud somewhere in the mine, and that their bodies would have to be dug out of the sludge. 'I just hope they didn't suffer,' she repeated endlessly. Then, as the temperature rose that morning, she started to rub her head and cried out, 'How much longer is it going to be? I just can't take any more of this.' As friends rushed to her side, she collapsed in a heap and had to be helped to the medical center. A check by Dr Mark Yaros, one of the local volunteers, found, not surprisingly, that her pulse and blood pressure were raised.

Her friend Tasha Stewart said a prayer to comfort her, and Leslie was laid out on a makeshift cot and given a sedative to calm her down. In her excited state she feared that she was going mad from the unrelenting pressure of not knowing what had happened to her husband and father. 'Please don't put me in a home,' she pleaded fearfully, recalling that a distant relation had never fully recovered after suffering a nervous breakdown. She believed that she too was teetering on the brink of nervous collapse.

Just at the moment when she seemed to be regaining her composure, her son Tyler, who was sitting by the cot, suddenly yelled out, 'There's Dad, there's Dad!' as Blaine's four-wheel-drive truck rolled into the fire hall car park, closely followed by his grandfather's car. Thinking that the families might need the vehicles, the mine company had decided to deliver them to the fire hall. It was a well-meant but ill-judged gesture, for the unexpected appearance of the cars only added to the agony of those waiting for news of the missing men.

The cars' arrival did little for Leslie Mayhugh's state of mind. Nor did the Governor's decision to limit the number of family and other supporters to just fifteen for each of the trapped miners. He agreed with volunteers and the clergy at the fire hall that the place was severely overcrowded. With drilling reaching a critical point, rescue workers expected to reach the men that day. All of them knew in their hearts that the result would be either elation or devastation. In either case, the families would need appropriate counseling, something that would be impossible in the atmosphere of busy turmoil that prevailed at the fire hall. 'I was trying to figure the scenario of how to react if bad news came down,' Father Jack O'Malley admitted. 'All hell would have broken out.'

The shortlist of fifteen placed further pressure upon the miners' families, since they had to decide who to choose and who to leave out, especially as a blood relation was not always as close or consoling as a friend. Already sorely tested, they now had to navigate this most awkward of social minefields at this most trying of times. Some people were bound to be offended if they were left off the list – and inevitably some did take offense. Others, tactfully, made the decision easier by volunteering to go. The members of the congregation from Sue Ellen Unger's church decided to leave the hall as a group, although they did not go far, gathering beneath the porch of a friendly Sipesville resident who lived next door to the fire hall.

Meanwhile, professional counselors were constantly on hand to shoulder some of the burden, focusing particularly on keeping the children entertained. A minister's wife brought her pet dog to play with the youngsters, but a suggestion to hire a clown to entertain them was vetoed as it was thought he would overexcite them. Puzzles and games were donated by local stores, and counselors were roped in, often against their better judgment, for the children's games. Tyler and Kelsey Mayhugh spent hours in the backyard searching for bugs for their pet chameleons. A counselor whom they knew as Tressa, who was terrified of insects and similar creatures, very reluctantly took one of the large spiders Tyler offered her from a polystyrene cup. 'I'm going to tell Blaine what I had to go through for you,' she joked later with Leslie.

It was something of a godsend that the children were being kept amused as events were moving apace at the drill site. As a result, John Weir's hourly briefings at the fire hall found an increasingly eager audience. 'I'm praying before you tell us what's happened,' Randy Fogle's mother would tell him each time he entered the hall. During the morning the second drill kept hitting voids, empty areas like air bubbles in the bands of rock. This was a real concern, for the command team feared that the drill might inadvertently puncture the bubble surrounding the trapped men, since it would be next to impossible to distinguish from the surface between these spaces and the actual mine. As a result drilling in the second rescue shaft was suspended at 188 feet, the effort now switching back to the first drill. By lunchtime on Saturday it had made excellent progress and had reached a depth of 224 feet into the rock – around twenty feet above the stranded miners.

It was just as well that the first drill, with its 26-inch bit, had gone so far, so fast. When the second drill resumed operations it lost its bit, hammer and reamer. The drill's operator, Larry Winckler, was distraught, tearfully telling John Weir during one of his hourly rounds, 'I really feel I failed you and I failed the people.' Weir hugged him and reassured him that he had failed no one. 'Larry, you were my success story because when drill Number One wasn't drilling you gave me what I needed to tell the people. You gave me those inches and feet. And to them people down there it didn't matter if it was Number One hole or Number Two hole. You were drilling when Number One was down and that's what people wanted to hear.'

During one of his briefings to the media that Saturday, Governor Schweiker tried to describe the mood at the drill site, acknowledging that the men were exhausted from their efforts, but utterly dedicated to bringing the men out alive. 'Their slogan is "Nine for Nine" – we're bringing up nine of our guys,' he said as he was whisked by his spokesman, David LaTorre, to yet another live TV interview.

Away from the media frenzy, both drill rigs were now silent. The Falcon rig was being repaired, and a decision had been made by Lauriski and the rescue team that the drill just above the miners should stop until the water had subsided to a level where there was no possibility of the men drowning when they broke through. As a result, the focus switched back to Dr Kelvin Wu's technical team, whose task now was accurately to calculate the volume of water being pumped out of the mine and assess its level inside the mine. Computing these figures with the necessary degree of accuracy called for cool heads.

Elsewhere, though, cool was in short supply that afternoon. John Weir came very close to losing his at one point while he was racing to complete his hourly round. As he drove to the fire hall to give the families the latest update from the drill site, his wife Cindy called on his cell phone to say that the TV news had just reported that the drillers had broken through. When he entered the fire hall an expectant buzz ran round the room, and family members demanded to know why he hadn't told them the news earlier. Incensed by this example of media irresponsibility, he explained that the news story was false. All at once he was surrounded by crestfallen faces, the hopeful looks fading to disappointment. 'I was just about ready to go back to my pickup, get out my pistol and blow that TV right off the wall,' Weir confesses.

As he walked out of the fire hall, the Governor and his entourage pulled up. When the mine company's spokesman told him what had happened, the Governor was furious, immediately ordering his press officer, David LaTorre, to drive to the media center and read the assembled journalists the riot act. Brushing aside protests from LaTorre, Schweiker warned, 'If there is one more false report, they are all outta here.' It was no empty threat. In a previous incarnation as the head of the Pennsylvania Emergency Management Agency, he had incurred the wrath of the media by ordering the arrest of reporters covering a storm and its aftermath.

The growing mood of antagonism was not helped when the local TV channel, Channel Six, gloomily reported that the Somerset morgue was too small to accommodate the nine miners if they were found to be dead. Instead, they would be taken to Johnstown. This was hardly likely to improve the morale of the rescuers working round the clock to bring the men out alive – or of the trapped miners' families.

In the sweltering heat of late afternoon, Joe Sbaffoni and his boss, David Hess, took the stage at the fire hall and did their best to cool down the expectations of the families and to prepare them for what would certainly be the most delicate stage of the operation. The miners' relations and friends – those left at the hall after the Governor's edict – still finishing off a buffet that had been donated by local restaurants, stood and listened as the two state mine-safety officials explained that drilling would not resume until the water level had dropped to the critical 1,829-foot level. They added that even after they had broken through to the miners, it would be some time before the rescue could even begin.

While retired miners in the audience nodded understandingly, Sbaffoni went on to explain that not only would the drill steels and bit have to be removed from the shaft, without compromising the air pressure, but that communications would have to be established with the men. All this would take several hours. As they left, they handed the microphone over to MSHA engineer Joe Tortorea, who had been told by his boss, Kevin Stricklin, that he was to be the fire hall's new master of ceremonies, deputed to inform the families of every development from the rescue site. At the front of the stage there was now a telephone connected via a hastily installed phone line to the command center. This was to be his hot line.

Joe, a fifty-nine-year-old supervisory engineer, admits that his heart sank when, at 4.00 p.m. on Saturday afternoon, he was told of his assignment. Like many senior officials participating in the rescue, he has attended numerous mine accidents during the thirty-one years he has worked in mining. Bitter experience has taught him that few rescue attempts are wholly successful. So when he arrived at the fire hall, he tried not to become too familiar with the anxious people there. He knew what a potentially explosive emotional situation he was walking into.

What he found heartening, however, was the number of people – volunteers, counselors, pastors and friends – who had come to Sipesville to support the families at their time of greatest need. They had clearly meshed into one close group in which, if a person faltered with the emotional burden they were carrying, others gathered around to support and nurture them. This, then, had become a community of caring, focusing on a positive outcome to their three-day ordeal.

Ironically, one of the first calls that came through on the hot line was from the sister of a miner who died in the 2001 Jim Walters mine disaster in Alabama, where an explosion killed thirteen men. Tearfully, she told the families that she was praying for the trapped men, and hoping that their loved ones wouldn't have to go through what she and others had endured. The message was something of a mixed blessing for a ripple of concern went through the waiting crowd as they realized that, in spite of the continuing flow of good news, the outcome of the rescue was by no means certain.

Indeed, throughout the county and all over the country, the unfolding story of the rescue had dredged up many painful memories in those who had been touched by previous mining tragedies. For pensioner Genevieve Wadas Komar from nearby

Johnstown, it rekindled thoughts of the day her brother died in a mine-shaft cave-in sixty-two years earlier. As if that were not tragedy enough, when her mother was told of her son's death she collapsed with a stroke and died a few days later. A thousand miles further west, Joy Ledger and Mary Bocook sat transfixed before their TVs, waiting for updates from the rescue site. The unfolding drama brought back memories of the day in 1984 when their husbands had died in Utah's Wilberg mine disaster. They knew only too well the awful helplessness of waiting. 'We were very tearful and it was very emotional,' said Ledger. 'It really brings you back to what it was like going through it. It was awful.'

Even inside the fire hall, the strained, expectant atmosphere stirred up other childhood memories. Father Barry Baroni, who had come to Sipesville to support the family of Dennis Hall, remembered how his own father, a miner, would come home from work, his face so black with coal dust that only his eyes showed. 'When he'd come in the door, my mother always gave a sigh of relief,' he recalled. 'Now, all these years later, I knew why.'

By the early evening the tension had become almost palpable, families hopeful but understandably apprehensive now that their seventy-two-hour vigil seemed to be approaching a conclusion. For the last three days their familiar refrain had been, 'How many feet and inches?' Now Joe Tortorea was ready to bombard them with figures. At 7.15 p.m. the engineer took to the stage in his unaccustomed role and announced that the water level was now at 1,829.33 feet – just a few inches away from the magic 1,829-foot level. Inside the Quecreek pit itself, miners were furiously operating the pumps, knowing that as soon as the water level dropped the drill could grind down to the trapped men. 'We are really close – really close!' a supervisor yelled at one gang of miners.

Just fifteen minutes later, Tortorea took another call on the hot line. Putting down the phone, he told his audience, now swelling as people came in from outside, that the water level was down to 1,829.21 feet. Slowly but surely the pumps were gaining ground. At the rescue shaft itself, the drill team had blown out water from around the bit and had added two more sections of drill steel, ready to recommence operations.

At 7.50 pm, Tortorea announced to cheers from his audience that the water level had now reached 1,829.08 feet, and that permission to begin drilling again had been given. Yet in the agonizing rhythm of this rescue, the families' spirits soon took a dip when, thirty minutes later, at 8.20 pm, they were told that an important seal on the drill had broken and that there would be a delay of between twenty and thirty minutes.

Although the drill had only gouged out another 2 feet of earth before it had been shut down – it was now at 226 feet – the good news was that the water level was now at 1,828.74 feet. As the families absorbed this news, a pastor from the local penitentiary said a few words, telling his audience that even the prisoners were praying for the trapped men.

At 9.00 p.m. drilling resumed, much to the relief of the anxious people in the fire hall. Almost on cue, the Reverend Mike Dunlap bounced on stage carrying two large containers of Brusters ice cream, which the company had donated to the miners' families. 'There must be a God,' he joked. 'Brusters are sending us ice cream.' In the overwrought atmosphere, his announcement came as a welcome relief. There was more. A few minutes later a jeep pulled up loaded with fifty or more boxes of pizzas, again donated by a local company.

Events were now moving rapidly. After a brief break at 9.15 for the drillers to remove rock shavings and slurry from around the bit, the drill had, by 9.50, powered down to 232 feet – 2 feet lower than the elevation at which the 6-inch drill had punched through to the miners three days before. At the rescue shaft, the drilling crews were as nervous as the families. Driller John Hamilton had a knot in his stomach as he pushed 'Rescue One' towards the trapped men.

By 9.50 the atmosphere in the hall as Tortorea announced that the drill team had hit the 235.5-foot mark was electric. Breakthrough was anticipated very soon. For the next twenty minutes there was a collective holding of breath as they urged the drill deeper into the earth. At 10.10 p.m. he announced that they were at 239 feet, and that the water level in the mine was dropping quickly. It was now at 1,827.92 feet elevation – a couple of feet below where, it was hoped, the men were crouching.

At 10.16 p.m. the hot-line phone rang in the hall. All conversation stopped. Picking up, Joe Tortorea listened carefully and then replaced the handset. He was joined on the stage by pastor Mike Dunlap. 'We have broken through into the roof of the mine,' announced a beaming Tortorea to his jubilant, wildly cheering audience. Performing on stage didn't get much better than this. One vital question was etched on everyone's faces, however. Were the nine men still alive?

No one had the answer. Yet.

At the rescue site, things were now moving fast. This was the moment they had all been waiting and preparing for throughout the last three days. Every action that would follow had been discussed and rehearsed, and all the necessary equipment and vehicles gathered and tested. Eighteen helicopters, including nine from the National Guard, were on standby, as were nine life-support ambulances; three well-practiced teams of stretcher-bearers were at the ready, and George Maxwell of the Enslow rescue team, who had been chosen as the first rescuer to go down the shaft, was primed for action. 'You put yourself in a zone,' he said of his state of mind at that moment.

Meanwhile, as the drill approached the breakthrough point, the men pumping water from the mine were herded out by safety supervisors, who feared that there was a remote possibility that poisonous gases might be released throughout the mine when the big drill broke through. No one wanted to take any chances. At the rescue site, the drill slowly and carefully ground its way through the remaining earth and rock so that it could make a clean break through the mine roof, the men operating the rig taking care that it would not crash through on to the miners.

A team of engineers and drillers were on standby to turn off a series of valves on the rig so that the pressure in the shaft, and thus in the mine itself, could be measured. This had been rehearsed frequently. The experts anticipated punching through at the 1,834-foot elevation. In the event, they broke into the cavern at 1,829 feet at 10.16 on Saturday evening. At that moment the order was given to shut down everything. The small airlock built by Larry Neff was placed over the drill and, for the first time in three days, the compressor feeding air to the trapped men was silent. Now John Urosek knelt by the shaft and took a reading with a pressure gauge. It registered normal atmospheric pressure. To double check he drifted chemical smoke over the opening. It moved only slightly, signifying that there was no escape of pressurized air from the mine. 'This was really exciting,' he said later. 'It meant that we did not have to spend hours decompressing them below ground. The pressure was normal.'

Next, Urosek measured the amount of oxygen, methane and carbon monoxide in the air underground. His detector told him that the oxygen reading was 20.4 per cent of atmosphere – the atmospheric oxygen content on the surface is normally 20.9 per cent. If it had been less than 19.5 per cent they would have turned the compressor back on and continued to pump good air down below.

As Urosek was completing his checks, driller Anthony Gibbons suddenly yelled out, 'Hey! Hey! They're tapping!' It was as though he had announced that they had struck oil; better, in fact, for it was the news that they had all been waiting for. A dozen men converged on the 6-inch drill, which was some 30 feet from the rescue shaft, one diving to the ground to press his ear against the pipe. For once this was no false hope. They could all hear three distinct bangs on the pipe, the time-honored signal used by miners trapped underground.

An MSHA official stationed by the 6-inch-drill site used his walkie-talkie to call the command center 200 yards away, and asked someone to come down quickly. Knowing that there was a small media pool in the vicinity, he did not want to say over the phone what he was calling about for fear of alerting the journalists. Everyone was conscious of Governor Schweiker's edict that the families had to be the first to know any news.

In the command center Kevin Stricklin listened to the terse message and, fearing that someone had been injured, hurried down to the drill site. As soon as he was told that tapping had been heard he raced back to the command center where his boss, Dave Lauriski, was briefing a woman aide to a local senator. Lauriski quickly excused himself and ushered his guest out, then gathered everyone in the room around him. 'We need to keep our wits about us and confirm what we have just heard,' he told them sternly.

At that point no one knew whether all the trapped miners were alive, or if any were injured. It was now imperative that they spoke to the miners before they informed their families or the wider world. Stricklin ordered State troopers not to let anyone into or out of the site. 'We would have looked pretty bad if we said we thought we heard pounding and said people were alive and then we didn't have them,' he recalls.

Once Urosek had given the signal that conditions underground were normal, the drill team managed by Louis Bartels was cleared to pull the drill steels from the ground. 'Tear it apart, tear it apart,' yelled Bartels as soon as he got the order to raise the drill. For the first time in three days they had a chance to find out what had really been going on twenty-four stories underground.

*

If John Unger could have seen Ron Hileman's face in the blackness, he would have found himself looking at a man grinning from ear to ear. 'You want to go home tonight?' Ron asked him. 'Yes, I wouldn't mind going,' replied Unger, in his quietly understated way. 'Well, grab your stuff – we found the hole,' he yelled. They had endured so many false dawns, so many times when they had imagined that they had heard a drill breaking through. Now it had really happened.

For hours now, the noise of the compressor delivering life-giving oxygen had drowned out the sound of drilling. The racket was, as one mine official said, like listening to six DJs playing rap music in your car.

Until the early afternoon the trapped miners had been able to hear the Number 2 drill grinding its way down towards them. Then it had fallen silent. They had not heard the Number 1 drill, which was driving through the ground some yards away from their position. It was only when Hileman and Tom Foy went on a scouting mission, guided by the dim light of their cap lamps, that they made their discovery. With the water level now much lower, they had gone to check on the 6-inch pipe which was some distance from their communal resting place. Suddenly everything went quiet in the cavern. The noise from above ceased. They pounded on the pipe to let their rescuers know that they were still around. Their three taps were answered by pounding from above. A few minutes later, with a rattle of gravel and debris, the pipe itself was pulled up from the mine chamber. Nearby they could see another much larger hole in the roof, made by the 26-inch drill. They had had to knock out one of the rough wall barricades they had built in a vain attempt to protect themselves from the water, to get a closer look. Now they knew rescue was close at hand.

They scuttled back to tell their friends, who were sitting in the pitch darkness, trying to stave off the cold and damp. Before he reached them, Hileman had yelled out the news, shouting at the seven others to follow him. They needed no second invitation, Blaine Mayhugh dropping his mining belt in the rush to the hole left by the 6-inch pipe. Thanking the Lord for deliverance they called up, 'Help, help – please get us out.'

This was precisely what the rescuers above aimed to do. Within thirty minutes of the breakthrough, all the drill steels were pulled out of the 6-inch shaft and at 10.53 p.m., Bob 'The Microphone' Zaremski knelt over the hole and dropped down a special two-way communications probe, containing a microphone and speaker, adorned with Day-Glo strips so that the miners could see it in the pitch darkness.

At first Zaremski had offered his headset to others in the rescue team, but this was his moment. They threw him a yellow hard hat and told him to get on with his job. As at the Saxman mine borehole, he crouched low over the shaft, covering himself with mud in the process, and repeated his stock phrases as the stainless-steel probe was lowered into the depths. 'Is anyone there? Can you hear me? Stay where you are.' The reason for telling the miners not to move was based on the assumption, resulting from the five-tap code heard on Thursday morning, that they had barricaded themselves in against the water.

Before his probe was more than 100 feet down the shaft, Zaremski thought that he could hear voices but, with the hub-bub of excited conversation at the surface, he couldn't be sure. About three-quarters of the way down, he definitely heard a reply to his question, 'Can you hear me?' It was the voice of John Phillippi saying, 'Yeah, we can hear you.' After two days of listening to the sound of dripping water through his headphones, Zaremski couldn't believe what he was hearing. He asked again. And again. Just to make sure, he asked, 'Are you the trapped miners?' It may seem a bizarre question, but as he now recalls, 'It was just disbelief, it was amazing to hear someone.' The expression of pure joy on his face told the rescuers all they needed to know. When he held up nine fingers, that just confirmed it. It was, he would say later, like kneeling to pray and having God talk back to you.

Phillippi now told him, 'We're all nine here.' Then, in a laconic aside that somehow symbolized the rugged humor and bravado of the men below ground, the miner added, 'What took you guys so long?' Standing over Zaremski was MSHA official Ray McKinney, who asked him to ask the men how they were. 'We're OK, we're fine,' came the reply. Taking over the microphone, McKinney told them, 'Hang on in there, we're coming to get you.'

It was now 11.10 p.m. and the news ran like wildfire around the site, rescue workers giving each other high fives, hitherto solemn, concerned faces breaking into huge grins. One rescue worker, conscious of the cameras and watchful eyes at the edge of the site, waved his arms in an effort to calm everyone down. For mine owner Dave Rebuck, standing just behind Zaremski, it felt as though the weight of the world had been lifted off his shoulders. Shakily, he and John Weir scrambled into a state trooper's car and roared off to Sipesville fire hall to tell the families.

As luck would have it, the police officer was new to the area. 'Do we go left or right?' he asked at the intersection of the road from the rescue site. Yet, even though he did not know the road, that did not stop him driving at high speed. As Weir recalls, 'His lights and sirens were going. I know we were traveling at over a hundred miles an hour when we passed Casebeer church. It has been a long time since I had been in a car going that fast. I told him; "Hey buddy, slow down, I don't want to get killed."'

In his excitement, the officer took little notice. As they reached a hump in the road before Sipesville village, his cruiser was traveling so fast that it went airborne, all four wheels leaving the tarmac, before he screeched to a halt outside the fire hall. Leaving an emotionally overwhelmed Dave Rebuck to make his way through the crowd, Weir pushed ahead, jumped up on stage and grabbed the microphone from Joe Tortorea. There was a brief pause, punctuated by a mutter of conversation as people wondered what this latest announcement would be.

Looking round the room, Weir asked for quiet. In a moment there was almost total silence. The only sound was the whirring of the two fans in the ceiling. 'Before I say anything, I want everyone to promise me that you won't go down to the rescue site.' They knew him by now, though they had never seen him like this before. This was the voice of a man who would brook no opposition. There was a ragged chorus of 'Okay, John', 'Whatever you say'. People were still streaming into the hall from the backyard and the carpark, and Weir was not satisfied. 'No, I mean this. I want every one of you to promise me that you will not go to the rescue site.'

This time there was a vigorous chorus of assent, rather like an audience being warmed up by a stand-up comedian. Except that Weir wasn't joking. 'Yeah, John, we promise', 'We give you our word'. He paused for a moment, gathering himself. Then, in a quavering voice, he announced, 'We have nine miners and they are all alive. And we are bringing them home.'

The room erupted. In the uproar, and with tears rolling down his cheeks, John Weir thanked God, and then his wife Cindy. 'It was such a great moment,' he remembers. 'Coal miners are the toughest guys in the world, but boy, that was something.'

He was not the only one with tears in his eyes. 'No one was ashamed to cry,' recalls Father Barry Baroni. 'People were screaming, jumping up and down, hugging each other all over the place. It was just the best news ever.' John Unger's twenty-five-year-old son, Stephen, said that he had never seen people so emotional, adding he had never cried so hard in all his life. The pastor from the local penitentiary shouted, 'Praise the Lord, praise the Lord!' His cries were taken up by others, their shouts resounding around the timber-built hall. Outside, people ran around, their arms waving in exultant celebration.

Amid the mayhem, Joe Tortorea was worried. He had not had confirmation himself from the command center. Reaching for the hot line, he called a colleague there, Ron Costlow, who told him that they had heard nothing. Tortorea was now very worried, concerned that John Weir, overwrought after virtually three days without sleep, had committed an enormous blunder. A couple of minutes later, however, his fears were allayed when the command center called and told him that nine men were alive and well. At last he too could join the celebrations.

Minutes after John Weir's dramatic announcement, Governor Schweiker and MSHA boss Dave Lauriski joined the jubilant throng at the fire hall. Their progress to the stage was like a victory parade, women hugging them and men patting them on the back, everyone showering them with a verbal barrage of praise and congratulation. Climbing up on to the stage, the Governor was smiling broadly as he told them what they already knew. Lauriski then explained that there would be some delay before the rescue capsule could be lowered down the shaft, as first the drill steels and the bit had to be removed. He assured the families that they would work as quickly and safely as was humanly possible to bring their loved ones home unharmed.

Then the Governor left to take the news to the world. Fifteen minutes later he bounded into the media center, wreathed in smiles. He cut a very different figure from the man who had stalked out of the Giant Eagle an hour earlier, his face like thunder. During a previous press conference, he had come to believe that he had been ambushed. As he was discussing the progress of the rescue, he was interrupted when one journalist, who was in contact with the rescue site, yelled out that the rescuers had established that the men were alive. His information was premature. Although the drill had indeed broken through, the men had not yet been contacted. After that, the Governor stonewalled questions for several minutes, refusing to confirm this latest report and leaving the assembled journalists irritated and confused. Moments after he left the podium he was seen dressing down officials, angrily accusing them of leaking information to the media. 'It got quite ugly,' one observer noted. 'Anyone would think that he was running for office and wanted all the glory.'

All that was forgotten when Schweiker, his fist punching the air in a victory salute, took the podium at 11.30 p.m. and told the waiting media, 'All nine are alive. Nine for nine. And we believe that all nine are in pretty good shape.'

An explosion of sound followed the announcement as jubilant journalists greeted the news with cheers, waving clenched fists in the air, their traditional cynicism cast aside until another day. 'Hallelujah, amen, thank God, thank God!' cried MSHA spokeswoman Amy Louviere, a leggy brunette who had spent the last few days briefing the media. Just a few minutes before the Governor arrived she had had to keep a poker face when a colleague from the command center had called to tell her that they had nine men 'alive and healthy'. Now she was overwhelmed by emotion.

She could, too, now share the moment with the media who, for once, were on the same side as the rescue team. The young reporter who had written the first story to appear about the Quecreek flood, Leona Kozuch, burst into tears, while TV news anchor Sally Wiggin broke down on air when she began to read from a wire-service bulletin that the miners were alive. She handed the copy to her co-anchor who finished reading from it. Even TV veteran Geraldo Rivera, who was broadcasting live from the Giant Eagle car park, was not immune to the mood of jubilation, kissing his women interviewees and hugging the men. He even called the Governor 'dude'. However, two female TV reporters who were seen shrieking and jumping up and down were severely chastised by their employers for failing to treat what was still a life-and-death situation with due gravity.

At Quecreek Number 1 mine itself, the men who had worked so hard to free their trapped workmates needed no excuse to celebrate. That night, two of the men who escaped the flood, Joe Kostyk and Ron Schad, were laying pipe for the pumps when a fellow miner started yelling that their buddies were alive. 'Everybody went nuts,' Joe remembers. 'Everybody was clapping and hugging and thanking each other. It was total happiness, like a huge weight had been taken off our shoulders. It seemed to be a miracle.'

Certainly they thought so, and were properly grateful. Joe, Ron and a few other miners formed a circle and said a prayer of thanks. Then, swept by a mood of exhausted elation, Joe put his arm over his friend's shoulder and said, 'Come on buddy. We're done here. Let's go home.'

Chapter VIII

RETURN OF THE PRODIGALS

FOR A TIME, it was like being on a rifle range down there. And almost as dangerous. Rocks, pebbles, gravel, dirt and caked mud hurtled down the shaft, slamming on to the mine floor and ricocheting around the ribs and roof. The trapped miners cowered beneath the fusillade. Mark Popernack was an early casualty, hit just beneath the eye by a piece of rock. 'It was like .22-caliber shots going off,' he recalled later. It had been bad enough when the drillers first took the drill steels out of the 6-inch hole and lowered the microphone. As they pulled out the whopping 26-inch drill, however, the volley of stones hurtling down the shaft became a bombardment. Nevertheless, the elation of their discovery and imminent rescue gave them renewed energy, and the nine men worked feverishly to build makeshift walls to protect themselves from the barrage.

At least, they now had proper lights to guide them for the first time in days. It was the first thing they had asked for, quickly followed by a request for chewing tobacco and snuff. The lights were lowered down the 6-inch hole almost immediately. Tobacco would have to wait. Besides the torrent of dirt and rock, the men faced a barrage of questions from above. Ray McKinney of the MSHA quizzed them about the condition of the air, whether they were in water and if they could make their way unaided to the rescue borehole. They reported that the air quality was fine, that the water was receding, and that there was a lot of dirt from the roof on the mine floor which they would clear before the 8-foot-tall rescue capsule arrived.

In the meantime, as the drill steels from the rescue shaft were being removed, Dr Richard Kunkle used Zaremski's equipment to question the men about their health. They replied that they had only one real concern, their crew chief, Randy Fogle, who was complaining of chest pains. 'That really made me nervous,' recalls Kunkle. 'I was concerned that he may be having an angina or heart attack.'

In the light of this, it was decided that Fogle would be the first passenger on the escape shuttle. Apart from John Unger, who had a painful shoulder, the rest of them were cold and wet but otherwise in reasonable condition – even Tom Foy with his history of heart problems. They would be in even better shape once they had that plug of tobacco. 'I was amazed how strong they sounded,' recalls Dr Jeffery Kravitz, who took turns with others to talk to the men while the rescue capsule was being prepared. 'They were calm, collected and joking around with each other.'

One of the first questions the trapped men asked was what had happened to the other miners who had been working in the Mains section on the night of the flood. It was something that had preyed on their minds for the last three days. Mine owner Dave Rebuck delivered the news they had all been waiting for. At first he joshed with them, saying, 'Where have you guys been? We've been looking for you.' Then he told them what they wanted to hear. 'Hey Denny, you're a hero,' he called down to Dennis Hall. 'You saved those guys with your phone call.'

The tears of relief they shed when they realized that their friends were all safe were tempered by genuine bewilderment when they heard that, above ground, the Governor, the

Assistant Secretary of Labor and around three hundred other people were working to save them. They were nonplussed as well to be told that they could not speak to their families just yet because there were so many media close at hand. With amused incredulity, they learned that presenter Geraldo Rivera, who had arrived in Somerset in a limousine, had just been unceremoniously kicked off a local farmer's land. Amid their laughter, however, there was astonishment that a major TV star like Rivera should come all the way from New York to Somerset County because of them. As Blaine Mayhugh was to say later, 'We maybe thought the story had made it to Pittsburgh.'

Away from the jokes and gossip, the nine men were instructed how to use the rescue capsule, and told what was going to happen to them at the surface. They were told that under no circumstances were they to try to exit the capsule themselves once they reached safety, and that, having been helped out, they would be taken by stretcher to be medically examined. They would also have to keep their eyes closed because of the bright arc lights that surrounded the rescue site, since their eyesight had been attuned to darkness for several days. To this group of tough individualists, all this seemed vaguely insulting. It was not the homecoming they had envisaged. The scene they had played out in their minds was one in which, once they reached the top, they would get showered, have a beer and a cigarette, grab a bite to eat, and go home. No fuss.

Unknown both to the rescuers and the trapped men, they were about to become the stars of a real-life reality show, their rescue televised nationwide, holding millions of Americans in suspense, as they anxiously watched the unfolding drama. When Governor Schweiker made his historic announcement that all nine were alive and well, he had also acceded to media requests that a single camera should be allowed to film the rescue live. The only condition he made was that the families of each of the trapped miners must agree first. With time at a premium, the Governor asked John Weir to call someone he trusted at the fire hall. Weir phoned his friend, the Reverend Mike Dunlap, and asked him to take a vote among the families, and let him know the result. 'If you lie to me, I will hunt you down and kill you,' he warned Dunlap. Fortunately, the minister realized that Weir, a great admirer of John Wayne, was acting out a scene from the western *Big Jake.* Or, at least, he hoped he was acting . . .

Dunlap went on stage and explained the situation to the families, saying that if they wanted to be able to see live coverage of the rescue in the fire hall, then it would have to be broadcast nationwide. Family members went into a huddle for a minute or two, before agreeing unanimously that the rescue should be televised. The decision was so last-minute that the rescue of the first two miners had to be taped and broadcast after the event.

While the camera was hastily being set up at the drill site, the rescue capsule, slung beneath a 40-ton crane, was loaded with everything the miners had requested: cap and lamp batteries, flashlights, drinking water, Hershey and KitKat candy bars, blankets, raincoats, glow lights, chewing tobacco, and two brands of snuff. The rescue team had also equipped it with an alarm to warn the miners of its approach, as well as with air-quality and air-pressure monitors and a headset linked to the team at the surface. The rescuers wanted there to be enough food and other supplies and equipment on the capsule so that if, as they had long feared, it dislodged a rock behind it on the way down, thereby blocking its passage back to the surface, then the men would have enough to keep them warm and nourished while the obstruction was cleared or, if that failed, the second rescue shaft was completed.

At 12.30 a.m. on Sunday, 28 July – just two and a quarter hours after rescuers had first cut through to the trapped men –

the capsule was ready to be lowered. Carefully and slowly the cage was unwinched into the mine. A few hearts missed a beat when it became snagged at the 170-foot mark – where the 30-inch hole narrowed to 26 inches – but its weight took it past the lip and it continued the journey to the bottom.

On the mine floor, the nine men unloaded supplies – falling on the chewing tobacco and candy – before helping Randy Fogle slide the capsule door upwards and ease his way into the cage. 'Get your butt in there and get the hell out of the mine,' was Blaine Mayhugh's less than deferential instruction to his boss. Clutching the white plastic bucket containing the notes that the men had written to their families in their most desperate hour, Fogle crawled inside the capsule, stood upright, slid the door shut, put on the headphones and adjusted the microphone as they had been instructed. He waved an ironical goodbye to his crew. 'See you at the top,' he said, a refrain that was taken up by the rest of the crew when it was their turn to leave their buddies behind. Then he spoke into the mike and the capsule jerked, steadied, and slowly began to move upwards until it was out of sight.

It should have been a fifteen-minute ride, but in the event the journey to the surface took half that time. This was just as well, for the tight-fitting capsule was claustrophobic and very wet, water from the underground stream running down Fogle's neck and back in spite of the rubberized raincoat he had put on. 'Won't this thing go any faster?' he yelled as the torrent splashed over him. On the way up he was asked his name, his medical condition, and reminded to keep his eyes shut at the surface and not to climb out of the capsule unaided.

At 1.00 a.m. on the Sabbath, after spending three days underground, a soaking, ink-black Randy Fogle arose from the rock tomb. Of his face, only the whites of his eyes shone out under the arc lights (the instruction to keep their eyes closed was almost impossible to obey). As the capsule came to rest, the scene resembled a tableau from the Scriptures, as countless arms reached upward, straining to help the exhausted miner out of the capsule. To an ecstatic and sustained roar of shouting, clapping and cheering, he was gently lowered on to the specially prepared metal litter. 'When I saw the smile on his face, that was my pay,' said one rescue worker. As the miner burst from the bowels of the earth, the imagery of rebirth, both physical and spiritual, was compelling. 'It was breathtakingly wondrous and akin to watching my children being born,' said an elated Governor Schweiker.

The six-man team carried Fogle from the drill site to the decontamination center as carefully and gently as if they were conveying a newborn baby. The presence of a state trooper on either side of the stretcher, guarding the route, reinforced the sense that this was indeed precious cargo. It was no accident. Not only had the stretcher teams tirelessly practiced the maneuver, but before the rescue cage was sent below SMRT leader Danny Sacco had warned the men not to let their excitement get the better of their teamwork. He even ordered one of them to change from shorts to long pants to give a more serious impression on national TV.

During the transfer, so smooth it looked choreographed, Dr Kunkle walked beside Randy Fogle, quizzing him further about his chest pains. At the decontamination site, the crew boss's clothes were unceremoniously cut away, and his entire body washed with detergent to get rid of the oily grime and tar that covered him; even his ears were sluiced out. The reason for all this was in case he needed to be placed in one of the nine highly oxygenated decompression chambers.

Afterwards, Kunkle and a US Navy doctor double-checked Fogle's medical condition. While a nurse inserted an intravenous drip to compensate for possible dehydration during his seventy-seven-hour ordeal, the two doctors checked his vital signs, including his heart rhythms, and blood and oxygen levels, as well as testing for any signs of decompression sickness. He was given the all-clear with regard to the bends, but there was concern about his heart rate. At one point it was racing away at 160 beats a minute. Most noticeable of all, however, was the fact that his body temperature was way below the normal 98.6 degrees. After three days living in a damp 55-degree atmosphere this was to be expected. As would be true of the rest of the miners, his feet, fingers and legs were mottled from immersion, the skin pale and wrinkled, as though he had spent too long in the bath. He was shivering and hot packs and space blankets were wrapped around him before he was transferred to a helicopter for the short trip to the Conemaugh Memorial Medical Center in Johnstown, where Dr Russell Dumire, a trauma surgeon, was waiting on the helipad. He was impressed to find his patient alert and talking, although rather bemused by all the fuss.

As Randy Fogle had disappeared out of sight of his crew below ground, Blaine Mayhugh joked, 'Okay, guys, now I'm next.' In fact he was just kidding, but the other guys didn't laugh. They told him that, because of the ages of his two young children, he should take the next shuttle to the surface. He needed no second bidding. He didn't have to wait long. Within fifteen minutes, the rescuers had removed the steel plate placed over the hole after the capsule emerged, marked its cable with spray paint, and sent it back on its way. Donning one of the raincoats, he waited for the capsule to reappear. When it did, he climbed into it, put on the headset, and ordered it to be hauled up. If anything, he found the ride worse than his boss had done. With the pouring water making breathing difficult, he shouted to rescuers, 'Get me the hell out of here! I mean *now!*'

When he reached the surface, everything seemed to blur into a haze of clapping, whistling and cheering rescuers and banks of intense bright light. He had one thought in his mind:

'I just wanted to see my wife and kids and my mom and dad,' he said later. As he lay on the stretcher, the Governor, having forged something of a bond with the miner's outspoken father, leaned over and told him that he had just seen his dad and that he had ordered him to get his son out of the mine. The news brought a smile to the miner's lips.

He would have found equally amusing the conversation of his wife and the rest of his family as they whiled away the time waiting for news of the first miner to be brought to the surface (the first live TV footage from the site showed the third miner being brought up). 'I'm going to kiss him to death, then kick his butt,' said his wife Leslie, as she anticipated their reunion. They speculated – correctly as it turned out – that a movie would be made of the saga and joked that if Joe Pesci or Danny De Vito were to play Tom Foy, then Blaine would want to have the tough-guy actor and wrestler known as 'The Rock' to take his part. Their mind-reading act proved uncannily accurate.

The jokes stopped, however, when Joe Tortorea announced that the first miner to come out of the mine had chest problems. Everyone looked at Denise Foy, thinking that it was her husband, Tom. When instead the name Randy Fogle was read out, everyone clapped and cheered, waving to his wife Annette and giving her and her family thumbs-up signs. In the commotion, she was approached by the Reverend Joseph Beer, who took her and her family outside and told them to which hospital Randy had been sent. As they got into their cars, Beer asked them to drive safely. In their haste and excitement, they left many of their belongings at the fire hall, as would most of the other family members who had camped there.

While the Fogle clan made their way to the hospital in Johnstown, Joe Tortorea announced the name of the second miner – 'Wayne Davis'. Everyone began to clap and cheer, but then stopped and began to look at each other quizzically. No one had ever heard of a Wayne Davis. Picking up the hotline phone, Tortorea checked with the command center. There had been a mix-up. A moment later he called out that the miner was in fact Harry Blaine Mayhugh. Leslie fell back in her chair, tears rolling down her face. She was so overcome with relief that at first she couldn't stand up and had to be helped to her feet by her sisters, Amy and Tonya. After pastor Beer told her that Blaine had been taken to Somerset Hospital, she immediately went outside and used her cell phone to call her cousin Brad, who lived near by and was looking after her children, Kelsey and Tyler. Then she was driven by her sister and brother-in-law, Pam and Tim McKinsey, to the hospital.

On the way they passed knots of people standing and cheering, blowing horns and waving makeshift cardboard signs with the phrase 'Nine for Nine' on them. Somerset County was spontaneously and exuberantly celebrating the triumph of faith and resolve over death and despair. For once, the good guys had won. All over America, the millions watching gave thanks for the miners' resurrection and their lives, many believing that they were witnessing a genuine miracle on live TV. The miracle also proved to be a ratings winner – CNN's audience, for instance, went up by an almost heavenly 629 per cent.

At the hospital, Leslie was relieved to learn that her father, Tom Foy, was the next man out. He was soon followed by John Unger, John Phillippi, Ron Hileman, Dennis Hall and Robert Pugh. The men, who chose the order of rescue themselves, were popping out of the earth at fifteen-minute intervals, confounding the planners, who had anticipated much slower progress. Indeed, in the case of the eighth miner, Robert Pugh, it took only four minutes for the cage to descend with two minutes on the ground and four minutes back to the surface – ten minutes in all.

For some of those waiting, however, the tension was almost unbearable. As each miner was brought out, young Lucas Popernack's face grew longer and longer, he and his brother

Dan becoming increasingly nervous as they waited for news of their dad. 'Why is he taking so long to get up?' Luke asked Cathy Custer, who was sitting with the family in the fire hall. 'Well,' she replied lightly, 'he's letting everyone who is sick come up first. Then he has to clean up the mine, pick up the blankets, sweep the floor and turn off the lights.'

She spoke more truly than she knew. For the second time during those three days, Mark was left on his own in the darkness. It had been his choice to take the last shuttle, and he told Dr Kravitz, who was guiding the men on their journey upwards, over Zaremski's voice link that he was relaxed about the idea. 'I know I will survive,' he said calmly. To keep him occupied, Dr Kravitz had asked him to use the gas sensors to monitor levels of oxygen, methane and carbon monoxide in the mine. The atmosphere proved to be normal, with no traces of poisonous gases.

While he crouched and waited for the elevator ride to freedom, this coolest of customers toyed with the idea of playing a trick on the rescuers by sending the yellow cage back empty. Then he thought better of it – apart from anything else, it would only take a rock to jam the shaft and he would be left below ground for who knew how long. A miner to his fingertips, before he climbed into the capsule he gathered up all the supplies and equipment he could manage to carry back up. 'There's a couple of caplights and candy bars in this duffle bag,' he said over the microphone. 'What do you guys want me to do with them?' As far as he was concerned, he was just a miner doing his job at the end of a rather long shift. 'You know what, Mark? – just get in and close the door,' he was told. Before he set off, his old school friend, Bill Arnold, joined in the teasing over the voice link, telling him to have a good look around to see if any of the others had left their wallets behind. In fact, Mark did bring back the atmospheric sensors, knowing how valuable they were. He was somewhat concerned, therefore, when he returned to the mine a couple of days later, to find that they were still with the clothes that had been cut off in the decontamination room and had not been returned to the mine manager.

When he reached the surface, Mark resigned himself to being manhandled out of the capsule and on to the stretcher. He knew he would become emotional when he got to the top, but he had not expected to be overwhelmed as he heard the scores of people clapping and cheering his arrival. All the miners would later struggle to describe that feeling; it was 'a miracle', 'the biggest day of their lives', just like the Fourth of July rolled into one with the Pittsburgh Steelers winning the Super Bowl. At the time, Popernack summed up his own feelings when he spotted Governor Schweiker helping to carry his stretcher. 'God bless America,' he said as he gave the thumbs-up sign.

Like Mayhugh and Hileman, who were considered fitter than the others, Popernack was taken by ambulance to Somerset Hospital after he had been checked by the doctors at the site. 'How are you doing, Doc?' he asked Dr Julie Bielec after he was taken out of the ambulance. 'No, I'm the one who should be asking how you are,' she told him. Like the other two miners, Dr Bielec and her team spent half an hour checking him over. While his wife and children waited impatiently to enter the emergency room, having driven to the hospital from the fire hall, once it was known that the last man was out, Mark Popernack was hooked to a warm intravenous drip to get his body temperature up and combat dehydration. The blankets, by now wet and cold, which had draped him in the ambulance were replaced with warm dry ones. His first request was for a large glass of milk – cool, naturally. (Indeed, an indication of the matter-of-fact way in which the miners dealt with their rescue is shown by one story that did the rounds of the two hospitals. It concerned a nurse who was filling out a standard-issue form for each arriving miner. As she went down the list, she inadvertently asked one of the men, 'Sex?' He replied dryly, 'Not for the last four days.') When his wife Sandy and children Lucas and Dan walked into the emergency room after Dr Bielec had finished her medical examination, the doughty miner began to cry as he embraced the family he had thought he would never see again. 'There wasn't a dry eye in the room, including mine,' recalls Dr Bielec. He was, however, composed enough to apologize to his pastor, Charles Olson, who had counseled his wife and family during their three-day ordeal and who now accompanied them into the emergency room. 'Reverend, I'm sorry I can't be in church this Sunday but I'll be there the next,' he sheepishly told the pastor of the Grace United Methodist church in Somerset, where the Mayhughs worship.

By the time Mark Popernack arrived at the hospital, Blaine and Leslie Mayhugh had shared the kiss that they had missed when he left for work on that fateful Wednesday. 'When I first saw him I kissed his hand and told him I loved him. I have never been happier,' Leslie recalls. As she walked through the door his first words were exactly what she wanted to hear. 'I'm never going back,' he said. Then he asked about the children. 'Oh, ask about the children, don't ask about me,' she joked, so elated to be with her husband again that she would not let go of his hand even when he drifted off to sleep. Like the other miners, his hands and legs were white and wrinkled because of his prolonged immersion in the icy water. Other than that, however, Leslie felt that he had scrubbed up a lot better than she had expected. It would, though, take another three showers before the sticky coating of coal dust and compressor-oil residue would finally be removed. The mental scars would take much, much longer to heal. 'It was like hell,' he told her. 'Worse than you can ever imagine. Pure, pure hell.'

At least Blaine was able to talk to his wife. John Unger had no such happy reunion. On advice from US Navy medics, he was placed in one of the Navy's decompression chambers from the rescue site when he arrived at the Conemaugh Medical Center in Johnstown. Doctors feared that the 'astronomical' pain that he was feeling in his shoulder might be a result of the bends rather than arthritis. For six hours he was kept in the highly oxygenated sealed chamber, which had been mounted on a flatbed truck parked at the hospital. The only way to see him was by climbing a flight of steps to the chamber and peering in through the observation window, while the only way to speak to him was via an intercom. His wife, Sue Ellen, could not manage the steps because of her multiple sclerosis, and proudly refused offers by nurses to manhandle her up the steps to see John.

Instead one of his first visitors was family friend Rona Hemminger, who climbed the steps and told him over the intercom, 'We love you. Hurry up and get home – the cows need [to be] fed.' Once he was released from the 'horrible' claustrophobic chamber, Unger wanted nothing more than simply to commune with his family and friends. He wanted to hug everyone, tell them how much he loved them and talk about the good times – good times that he had thought he would never experience again. While he answered questions about those three terrible days in the black cavern, it was not something he wished to dwell on. The experience was still much too raw. As he hugged his daughter Vikki, his son Stephen, who had feared that his father would never come home, joked, 'You just had to prove me wrong and get out of there.' There is more than a grain of truth in the remark, for it was that sort of determination that helped Unger and his workmates.

Like John Unger, Tom Foy was eager to put the nightmare behind him. Once blankets heated to 140 degrees had taken away the chill – the body temperature of the coldest miner was found to be 92.5 degrees – he had one thing on his mind when he got to hospital: a decent plate of food. Doctors, who were concerned about the bouts of chest pain he had suffered underground, especially as he had a history of heart problems, had wanted to keep him on a bland diet.

It was not long, however, before he was back to his ebullient best, berating the hospital staff for trying to feed him soup and green jelly sandwiches. 'I want real food,' he complained. 'I don't care if my heart explodes.' It was another twenty-four hours before he had his wish – a huge plate of pork, spaghetti and mashed potatoes, with ice cream to follow. (Indeed, the next day even the Governor got the Tucker treatment. When he visited Foy in his room at the hospital, the excitable miner told him to 'make it quick' as he wanted to watch the NASCAR racing on television.) That first night, though, with his wife Denise smiling on indulgently, the starving miner wolfed down donuts, sandwiches and fizzy pop. Like the rest of them, he also craved his chewing tobacco which was now arriving by the boxful at the hospital as word got out that this had been one of the miners' first requests. The doctors allowed them their chew, but drew the line at orders for cold beers.

In fact, when Robert Pugh, who was in a nearby room, had got his first belt of chew after it had been sent down to them in the mine, the nicotine buzz had made him dizzy. By now, he was dizzy with the emotion of seeing his children, Jessica, Julie and Ben, and his girlfriend Cindy, who throughout her vigil in the fire hall had carried his favorite shirt with her. 'I'm the type of man who doesn't cry at all,' Pugh said. 'I couldn't help it when I saw my kids at the hospital. I bawled hard that day.' Just to make sure that he was not dreaming, he stayed up all night to watch the sunrise. 'After being in the dark that long I just wanted to make sure I was alive, see the daylight,' he said simply.

The first fingers of daylight were spreading across the drill site before the rescue teams had properly sorted out their equipment. As Bill Arnold wearily milked his herd, the men who had made it all happen relished the moment. At his last media briefing at 3.30 that morning, the Governor had been voluble in his praise for their efforts. Like the scientists and engineers who brought Apollo 13 back to Earth after its space mission went awry, the rescuers were the unsung heroes of this incredible operation. 'I wanted to sit back and enjoy it,' Kevin Stricklin remembers. 'This was history, and I knew I would never see this again in my life. If I could have bottled the feeling, I would have.'

Everyone felt the same tremendous lift. When he arrived at the command center trailer after saying goodbye to the assorted volunteers and clergy at the Sipesville fire hall, Joe Tortorea went over to Stricklin and thanked him for giving him the assignment of his life. 'It was like experiencing my wedding day, the birth of a child and winning the lottery all at the same time,' he told everyone, tears rolling down his cheeks. They knew exactly what he meant. That morning, no one's eyes were dry. 'I still can't stop crying,' says Joe Sbaffoni, who was greeted by the sign 'Thanks Joe' when he arrived to play for his softball team later that day.

The word 'miracle' was never far from anyone's lips as they celebrated this unique confluence of providence, prayer and physics, the drama strengthening not only their faith in themselves, but their religious beliefs as well. 'Our Lord Jesus Christ was the tenth man down there,' says MSHA engineer Gerry Davis. 'I give Him the glory. He wrote the script and we were His instruments.'

Dawn was breaking by the time engineer John Urosek swung into the driveway at his home in Connellsville in Fayette County, an hour's drive away from the rescue site. In the first frantic hours of the rescue, he was the man who came up with the inspired idea of creating an air bubble that held back the floodwaters from the trapped miners and brought them breathable air. By now he knew from the miners themselves, via their conversation with Ray McKinney, that that decision had saved their lives. It was knowledge he would savor for ever. He smiled as he saw the 'Nine for Nine' poster on the front lawn, anxious to tell his wife Claudia about the incredible events of the last four days, and about his role in the drama. Eagerly he launched into his story. Midway through a sentence, the exhausted engineer promptly fell asleep. If ever there had been a job well done, this was it.

Chapter IX

HI HO, HI HO, IT'S OFF TO DISNEY WE GO

I N HIS PRESSED blue slacks, striped belt and smart short-sleeved shirt, Ron Hileman looked for all the world as though he had just stepped off the golf course. He seemed fit and well, his manner confident and hearty, and there was a lolloping swagger to his walk. With his questing look and bushy but neatly trimmed gray beard, it was easy to understand why he had the nickname 'Hound Dog'.

As he embraced miner Gerry Mills – like Hileman, also a roof bolter – at the entrance to the Quecreek mine, it seemed as though he had just returned from a relaxing holiday – until he started talking. 'Jeez, it's good to see you,' he said. 'We thought you guys were gone. We just prayed and prayed for you.' Mills quickly corrected him, saying that he was not one of the nine miners who had escaped the flood. As luck would have it, he had been on another shift that day. He added that he was 'darn glad' to see his buddy, and gladder still that he was safe and sound.

'Glad?' said Hound Dog. 'Glad? It's a hell of a lot bigger word than glad.' Then he began to talk, reliving the awful hours when he and his coworkers had frantically built barricades against the flood, only to see every one of them washed away. 'Oh man, oh man,' he said, shaking his head in remembrance. This was still too painful, too raw. It would be some time before he could tell the story over a couple of beers at Gabo's Bar, the miners' regular hangout in Stoystown. Seeing his wife Cathy and their grown-up children becoming restless as they waited in his pick-up, he patted Gerry Mills on the shoulder. 'Thanks, buddy,' he said before heading off to the mine to show his family the scene and to thank all the men who had helped him to see the sun and breathe the air of this day.

Up the road, at the rescue site John Phillippi and his wife Melissa were greeting some of the drillers who were clearing and cleaning the site. They posed with them for group pictures, delighted to be with the men whose muscle, skill and toil had helped save John's life. On the way to the site they had noticed a spontaneous flowering of roadside signs, some in neon, some printed, some handwritten, praising and thanking God for the miracle and congratulating the miners and their rescuers. A little earlier Tom Foy, the last of the nine to come out of hospital due to his heart condition, had also visited the site to see and marvel at the miracle of his rescue. He was spotted by MSHA engineer Gerry Davis, who earned a bear hug of gratitude from the diminutive miner when he realized the part Davis had played in saving his life.

Earlier, when the men had gathered to face the phalanx of media at their first press conference in the parking lot at the Conemaugh Memorial Medical Center in Johnstown on Monday, 29 July, they had made it clear that they were there as much to praise the rescuers as to tell their incredible story. 'I came today to thank everybody out there,' said John Unger. Typically, he added, 'I thank our Lord God Almighty.'

On 4 August, a week after their great escape, an interdenominational thanksgiving service at the Casebeer Lutheran church, just yards from the rescue site, gave the miners a chance to meet

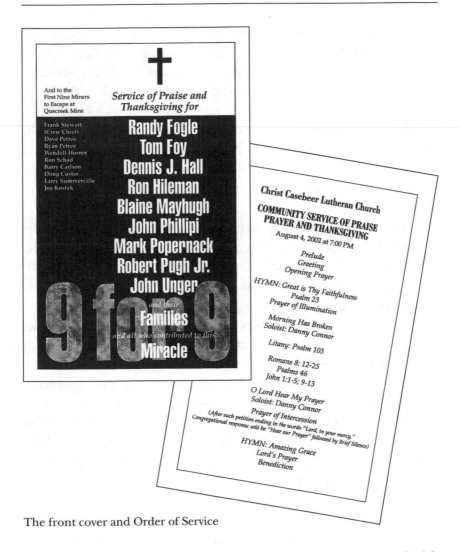

The front cover and Order of Service

some of the rescuers for the first time and to be reunited with the friends whom they had feared they would never see again. During the forty-minute celebration, which was transmitted live on CNN, the rescued men were commended for their strength and teamwork, while those who escaped were praised for their vigilance. The reading of Psalm 40 – 'I waited patiently for the Lord, he turned to me and heard my cry. He lifted me out of the slimy pit, out of the mud and mire, he set my feet on a rock' – was seen by many as entirely fitting to this epic struggle. After the service, at which, among others, Father O'Malley and the Reverends Doebler, Beer, Dunlap and Ritenour presided, the reaction of John Unger when he saw escaped miner Joe Kostyk may have lacked the poetry of the psalm but was just as heartfelt. 'I didn't think I would ever see your ugly face again,' he said as he hugged his friend. There were hugs aplenty as two bands of brothers were reunited; hugs, too, for relations and other well-wishers.

While their immediate human response was to give thanks to those who had saved their lives, the nine miners, buried from the world for four days and then sequestered in hospital, would need time to appreciate fully the enormous impact their dramatic rescue had made upon the rest of the community and upon the country at large. Their story was not just that rarest of events, a life-and-death struggle with a happy ending; it became clear, as the details percolated out, that it was also a tale of courage, comradeship and endurance that harked back to another, more innocent, time, their selflessness and unassuming heroism seeming to prove that the age of chivalry was not dead. If anything, the miners were incredulous when people commented upon the way they had stuck together in adversity. For them, to do so was as natural as breathing and just as unremarkable.

Had they had time to read the newspapers, which none of them did as they caught up with sleep, family and friends, they would have discovered a world intrigued by, and admiring of, their modest bravery and down-home values, particularly their unwavering faith in God and the importance they attached to family life. At times, the gush of tributes, some bordering on the glutinous, seemed almost as forceful as the water that had threatened to envelop them days earlier. Crew chief Randy Fogle agreed with me when I suggested that the week before they had been up to their necks in water, and now they were in danger of drowning in bullshit. 'That's about right,' he said, a hunk of ever-present chewing tobacco in his mouth.

Many of the commentaries made valid points, however. An editorial in the *Philadelphia Inquirer* captured the prevailing mood, its author writing that the nine miners had given the nation 'a new lesson in tough': 'Main rule: You stick together, literally tie yourselves together; when one of you falters, the rest give support. The weakest link isn't someone to be abandoned, but rather someone to be encircled and hugged. Tough also means you aren't embarrassed to pray, to cry. But you resist the tendrils of fear and desperation, because that might affect the rest.'

One commentator, Jim Klobuchar, writing in the *Christian Science Monitor*, focused on the contrast between the miners' story and the mood in the rest of America. 'It was the realization through the homes and streets that in an exasperating time in America – stock market turmoil, corporate crookedness, politicking, and shadows of the terror attacks – here was an hour when, together, millions of people could feel the exhilaration of the transforming strength of hope.' The contrast between the 'me-first' ethic of corporate America and the selflessness of the miners, who were now coming to be seen as representing the traditional values of the nation's heartland, was illustrated in a pithy syndicated cartoon in the local Johnstown *Tribune Democrat*. This depicted a group of CEOs in hard hats standing atop the mine. One says to another, 'They're stuck 240 feet below the surface.' The other replies, 'What's in it for us?'

The miners' ordeal and their rescue had also clearly struck a nerve worldwide. The letters pages of local newspapers filled with messages from as far away as Heidelberg, Germany, Perth, Western Australia and Canada, praising the men for their strength, courage and compassion. 'You showed what the American spirit truly means,' wrote one well-wisher, while a local bank took out an advertisement which read, '240 feet of solid rock is no match for the strength of this community.'

That strength was a theme taken up by President Bush when he met with the miners and many of their rescuers at a volunteer fire station in Greentree, Pittsburgh, on 5 August, just eight days after the incident. The nine miners, casually dressed in jeans and T-shirts, sat on a raised platform as the President spoke, saluting them as men of the 'right stuff'. He praised their self-reliance, and their determination to stick together and to comfort each other. 'What took place here in Pennsylvania really represents the best of our country, what I call the spirit of America, the great strength of our nation.'

While they were delighted to meet the President, and enjoyed chatting to him once the formalities were over – he even signed Lori Arnold's ankle cast – they felt increasingly awkward and uneasy about the attention they were attracting. For men used to working in the dark, the glare of the media spotlight was becoming almost intimidating, as well as unwelcome. 'This is not really me,' said John Unger as a clutch of microphones was shoved in his face. 'I'm just a common man.' As far as John Phillippi was concerned, he just wanted to get out of there and go fishing with his kids. Hileman said, 'You know, I'm just a good ol' boy from the country. I'm not expecting this kind of thing, this is very overwhelming,' and several of the other miners said much the same.

Yet all nine were on a celebrity roller-coaster which, try as they might, they could not get off, or not, at least for the moment, while the interest in them was still firing the media. The first to appear before the cameras were Blaine and Leslie Mayhugh, who were interviewed at Somerset Hospital on Sunday, 28 July, just hours after Blaine had been pulled from the mine. His admission that, for the first time, he had failed to kiss his wife before going to work on Wednesday, and Leslie's obvious and tearful relief at having him back safe, struck a sentimental chord with viewers. There was a positive by-product, however. Since Leslie was wearing a University of North Carolina baseball cap, college officials contacted the couple and offered their children scholarships. Later they sent T-shirts and caps for the family.

Everyone and everything touched by the miracle was sprinkled with the holy water of celebrity. While Governor Mark Schweiker, who was quick to announce an official inquiry into the inundation, appeared on the *Jay Leno Show*, the elderly yellow rescue capsule was clocking up more TV time than a chat-show host. Like some medieval religious relic, it was paraded around the country, first the star attraction at a mine-rescue contest in Reno, Nevada, and then the subject of a metaphorical tug of war between the 'nation's attic', the venerable Smithsonian Institution in Washington, DC, and a local coal museum in Windber, Somerset County, as to which should have it as an exhibit. When it seemed that the Windber Coal Heritage Center had won the tussle, it announced plans to exhibit other relics from what was now known as the 'Miracle at Quecreek': the blue Hawk Mountain sport shirt the Governor had worn when he announced that the men were alive; the quarter-size brass tags that miners use to show who is in and out of the mine; as well as survey stakes, the light first sent down to the trapped men, and helmets and clothing they had worn. Other collectors offered Ron Hileman hundreds of dollars for his helmet, while an Internet auction saw copies of a special edition of the local *Daily American* sell for $7 each, and a miner's pail, unrelated to the incident, go for more than $700.

In the face of the tidal wave of publicity, the miners behaved as they had when the flood broke underground – they stuck together. When NBC's *Dateline* show asked John Unger for an interview, he agreed on the condition that correspondent Stone Phillips came to dinner at his farm home and then only if the interview was with all nine miners. The deal was done, the

Phillips interview proving to be a model of the genre, as he carefully coaxed the story out of the nine men, who, less than a week after their rescue, were still in a state of shock, and wholly unused to articulating their thoughts and feelings in front of blazing camera lights. As they recounted the details of their seventy-seven-hour ordeal, it came as no surprise to the millions who watched the program when all of the men except Dennis Hall said that, for the sake of their families, they would never return underground.

That refrain was repeated when Blaine Mayhugh told David Letterman on air later that week that he would never go back to mining. Although Blaine was nervous at the idea of appearing alone on his favorite TV show, he had reasoned that it would afford a once-in-a-lifetime opportunity for Leslie and the children to see New York. At the top of their wish list were trips to the Statue of Liberty and 'Ground Zero', the site of the World Trade Center atrocity. When they arrived in New York they were given the full VIP treatment – greeted with a stretch limousine, installed in a plush hotel suite, and handed $500 spending money for their stay. It was also the first time Leslie and the children had flown anywhere. The young miner walked on stage to a rapturous ovation from the audience, and proved to be such a hit that Letterman asked him to stay on for longer than had originally been scheduled.

It was afterwards that the fun really began. They went to a comedy theater hoping to watch the show in quiet anonymity. It was a vain hope for the theater management had been alerted to Blaine's presence. During one comedy act he was called on stage and found himself in a dance contest with seven other members of the audience, strutting his stuff to the 1970s disco hit by Wild Cherry, 'Play that Funky Music White Boy'. Inevitably he won. It was hard to imagine that this was the same man who, less than a week earlier, had scribbled a farewell note to his loved ones.

For the Mayhughs and the rest of the miners, those first few days after their rescue went by in a haze. Exhausted, traumatized and overwhelmed, in a matter of days they had gone from the possibility of a terrible death to swapping jokes with the President. Yet the nation wanted the miners to have their fifteen minutes of fame – and a few more. So too did the Hollywood agents who flew into Pennsylvania hours after their rescue, looking to sign up the miners for a movie. Just for their stories alone, Blaine Mayhugh and his father-in-law Tom Foy were rumored to have been offered $1 million by Warner Brothers. They refused, saying that they had stuck together down the mine and that they would continue to do so on the outside. 'We have a bond right now that no one else can ever experience,' Tom Foy remarked.

Just as he had led them during their perilous days down the mine, Randy Fogle now agreed to shoulder the burden of any commercial negotiations, even though he found the constant phone calls from agents, journalists, TV producers and promoters wearisome. 'It's getting to my wife and kids and it's getting to me but I said I would do it and I will,' he said. He replaced a young local lawyer, Jim Courteney, who had initially been asked for advice, with a Pittsburgh attorney, Thomas Crawford, who had once represented a friend of the Fogle family.

The lawyer sifted through more than 120 proposals and quickly realized that the powerful ICM agency had already signed Bob Long, the surveyor who had used a GPS system to pinpoint where to drill the life-saving 6-inch hole. It seems that the miners decided to throw in their lot with him, probably fearing that a split deal could affect their earning potential. In the end the nine miners and the rescuer signed a $1.5 million deal with Disney and ABC for a TV movie provisionally scheduled for Thanksgiving in the coming November. Upon reflection, however, several of the miners later came to feel that they had been railroaded into an agreement, forced into a corner by Long's existing arrangement. In the beginning, however, most of them, confused by the bewildering array of offers cascading down upon them, were untroubled by talk that, after tax and lawyers' fees, the $150,000 they would each receive would not provide shelter from too many rainy days for the miners, eight of whom had now decided to leave mining. As far as John Unger was concerned, if he had enough to put a deposit down on a new John Deere tractor, he was happy.

Over the weeks, a sense of dissatisfaction began to grow, spilling over in early September when seven of the miners took their attorney, Thomas Crawford, to court, claiming that he had not paid them any of the money from the Disney/ABC deal. The issue had been sparked when Blaine and Leslie Mayhugh tried to buy a new family car, only to discover they had insufficient funds in their bank account.

At a courtroom hearing in Somerset, Judge Eugene Fike heard evidence to the effect that Crawford had apparently been so dilatory in financial matters affecting the miners that Tom Foy was 'thinking of going and sitting on the doorstep of Mr Crawford's office to personally get the check he felt he was entitled to'. As a result, Crawford signed a consent decree undertaking to pay the money he owed, less his legal fees. In the end, Randy Fogle and Mark Popernack opted to stay with Crawford, while the others hired a new legal team.

By now, the miners realized that, as one commentator put it, they had signed away their rights to everything but their DNA when they joined forces with the giant Disney corporation. The aim of their new lawyer, Steve Reich, whose clients include ice-hockey star Mario Lemieux of the Pittsburgh Penguins, was to exploit any loopholes in the Disney contract in order that the miners – or the seven for whom he acted – could make independent endorsement and sponsorship deals. 'I want to make sure the miners never have to go underground again,' Steve Reich said.

While Reich examined marketing possibilities, a second attorney, Howard Messer, investigated the circumstances surrounding the Quecreek mine inundation. Given the fact that under America law the mine owner, Black Wolf, is exempt from any liability, Messer and his team were trying to establish who was actually been operating the Saxman mine before it closed in 1964. The discovery of a map in the archives of the Windber Coal Heritage Center, which showed different boundaries between the Quecreek and Saxman mines from those in the map used by Black Wolf, added spice to the pursuit. 'It's going to be a hard job,' admitted Messer.

Although dissatisfaction over the financial deal was undoubtedly of growing concern, the nine miners were united in their desire to ensure that the movie should do nothing to embarrass the county, their fellow miners, and the many rescue workers and volunteers who selflessly worked for their release. Such was their anxiety to ensure that the story was told properly that they were prepared to upset their families and go back down a mine – 'just for a couple of days' – to show the film's directors and actors how miners work.

On 5 August, the day on which they met President Bush, they had agreed to judge a kind of 'beauty contest' of possible producers for the film, whom Disney executives had lined up in a Pittsburgh hotel, so that they could be sure that the producer eventually chosen would understand their concerns. Of the six contestants, the miners gave the rosette to movie veteran Larry Sanitsky, not just because, in his jeans and gray Gap T-shirt, he looked like them, but because he had been down a mine when he produced *Act of Vengeance*, a story about corruption in the miners' union.

While news of a TV movie about the 'Quecreek Nine' sent a ripple of excitement through Somerset County – more than 700 people attended an open audition for extras to take part in the film – other voices urged caution. Even before the ink was dry on the deal, SMRT co-founder Danny Sacco expressed his concern that, because the rescue was a triumphant team effort, to single out just a handful of people might marginalize the others, demeaning the importance of their contribution. The Black Wolf Company's spokesman, John Weir, a friend of Randy Fogle, was more outspoken, commenting scathingly on the fact that technician Bob Long had won a slice of a financial arrangement which, in Weir's opinion, should only have involved the nine miners. 'Everybody is upset that they paid this guy and he didn't do dick shit,' Weir said angrily. 'Anybody could have done what he did. We just gave him the coordinates. He couldn't find his ass with both his hands.'

Early indications that the Disney movie would capture the selfless spirit of the rescue were not encouraging. Bill Arnold, a mild-mannered man who had earned the respect of rescuers and rescued alike, was contemptuous of the behavior of some Disney executives. He complained bitterly after they offered him a mere $2,500 to spend days filming on his farm. When he refused the offer, a Disney representative told him, 'I don't care and neither will America if the rescue was not shot at the actual rescue site. All we need is a hole in the dirt.' Instead, they chose a farm several miles from the actual site as the location for the filming of the rescue operation.

Like most people involved in the rescue, it was not the derisory financial incentives that offended Arnold, but the way in which the film script, in his eyes, caricatured those who took part. In real life, when the men were first trapped underground, he had taken his pistol with him when he went to confront the unknown intruders roaming around his land with flashlights. When he realized that the men, several of whom he knew, were trying to locate a drilling point in order to reach the trapped miners, he did all he could to help. As a result, he objected when he found himself portrayed in the script as a 'backwards hillbilly' who pulls out his .45 and orders the men to freeze or else he will shoot them. 'I hope they have taken those scenes out,' he says. Arnold is currently in talks with movie directors about a rival film which, he feels, will be a more fitting tribute to all those who gave of themselves in order to save others.

There were unfortunate precedents for all this. Indeed, the legacy of bitterness surrounding the TV movie about a baby named Jessica McClure, who in 1987 was rescued from an abandoned mine shaft by paramedic Robert O'Donnell, was a salutary reminder of how celebrity and community rarely mix. Her rescue, played out in the full glare of the media spotlight, enthralled the world but split the town of Midland, Texas, where she lived. At issue was how the rescuers were to be portrayed in a TV movie. Municipal workers wanted one producer; volunteers another. It escalated into two months of bickering that split the very community that Jessica was supposed to have united. Tragically, in 1995, O'Donnell shot and killed himself, his brother Ricky saying that his life 'fell apart' because of the stress of the rescue, the attention it created, and the anticlimax of everyday life. He became addicted to fame.

The parallels with the situation surrounding the Quecreek rescue were enough to cause comment. Sergeant Andy Glasscock of the Midland, Texas, police warned the miners to stay away from 'damn Hollywood' and just enjoy having their lives back. Of the McClure incident, he recalled, 'Everybody got the big head. Everybody was somebody. We were just little country guys doing our job. Then the movie contract divided us up.'

In Somerset County, the communal wounds seemed to be opening up the moment Blaine and Leslie Mayhugh arrived home after their first trip to New York. It had been a turbulent flight – Leslie vowed never to fly again – but what they came home to proved far more upsetting. Among their mail was a letter castigating the miners; 'Get over this. Get on with your life. It's over,' was one of its less disagreeable comments. For two pages the unsigned note continued in a similar vein, much of it envious and rather pathetic. It was the first – and mercifully the last – such letter received by the couple. Even so, it was unnerving and they passed it on to the police. 'I didn't ask to be put in this position,' Leslie told concerned friends. Elsewhere, a relative of one of the miners, who asked not to be named, was given a written warning by her employer for spending too much time on domestic business during the rescue. 'No one died. Move on, get over it,' her boss told her.

On the surface, further signs of fractures in the close-knit community were becoming apparent even before the service of thanksgiving at the Casebeer Lutheran church on the first Sunday after the rescue. Several of the escaped miners' wives approached journalists, to whom they handed out leaflets and two poems, written by Kathy Petree, whose husband and son escaped the torrent. The badges the women wore on their dresses and the poems bore the same legend: 'The Forgotten Nine', followed by the men's names. The women were anxious for the world to know that their loved ones had suffered greatly as a result of the flooding of the Quecreek mine.

If the Forgotten Nine felt that their hardships had been ignored, in the days to come they were to feel not just neglected but positively slighted. After the church service the miners and their families went to Sipesville fire hall for a private reunion. There the organizers handed out ninety cases of beer, ten for each of the rescued miners. It was only when miner's wife Diana Schad pointed out that there had been eighteen miners working together that night that the allocation was revised, each miner receiving five cases. On the following day, all eighteen miners went by coach to Pittsburgh to see the President. While organizers allowed the rescued miners to bring their families, the men who had escaped had to go alone, even though there was ample room at the Pittsburgh fire station. On arrival, they were seated at the very back of the room, unremarked and virtually unacknowledged. As one of them said, 'It was just a long boring bus ride.' The final straw came when a reporter asked Joe Kostyk if he felt jealous of the Quecreek Nine. As he recalls, 'If the Secret Service hadn't been there I would have punched him out. That was the dumbest, most insulting thing I have ever heard. We weren't jealous of them, we were happy for them.'

What concerned them most, however, was the suggestion, made in several news reports, that, after being alerted to the danger by Dennis Hall, they had run out of the mine, and then taken a shower and gone home. Nothing could have been further from the truth. In the end, it was not the Disney deal, or the money, or the fleeting celebrity that infuriated them, but the implication that they had let their buddies down – that, when disaster stuck, they had cut and run. This was an insult not only to them, but to their values and their community, the negation of an ethic that outsiders, particularly the mass media, could never appreciate. How could they? In dealing with the miners, they were dealing with a world in which comradeship and loyalty meant far more than fame and money.

Joe Kostyk reflected the group response of the men who escaped when he said, 'For all the money in the world I would not go through what they [the trapped miners] went through and that's the honest-to-God truth. Those guys have been nothing but great. My buddies know that we didn't run out on them. They know that we were all there until the end no matter what the outcome was. That's good enough for me. The rest of it, that does upset me.'

Whether by luck or good judgment, the organizers of events involving the miners began to get the message. Moreover, unlike the rescue of Jessica McClure in Texas, the miracle at Quecreek served to strengthen rather than diminish the community, the eighteen men banding together against those, whether media or event organizer, who failed to appreciate the brotherhood of mining. In the weeks following the flood it was the eighteen miners as a group who were invited to meet the Pittsburgh Steelers at the team's training facility, who dedicated an outsize American flag to Bill and Lori Arnold at their farm as a gesture of thanks. It was also all the miners who were guests of honor at the annual Somerset County Fair on 18 August, paraded round the ring, to huge applause, in a covered wagon pulled by Butch Lepley's Belgian draft horses.

Parades and pageants aside, what really connected the eighteen miners, like men returning from war, was the shattering ordeal they had gone through, an experience even other miners and their families can never truly share. All were touched, some traumatized, by the trial by water. For them, the words 'post-traumatic stress disorder' is more than just a glib phrase. Night times are worst. 'When he is sleeping, he calls out,' said Diana Schad of her husband's reaction to his narrow escape from a horrible death. 'He hears the water and the thundering of the walls caving in and the splashing. The water coming directly behind him and engulfing him. He's not alone. All of them are going through the same.' While he was laying pipe for the pumps inside the mine during the rescue attempt, Ron got the shakes when a two-man golf cart went swishing through water in another section, the sound bringing back terrible memories of that awful night.

Like some of the others, Robert Pugh stays up late into the night so that he is so exhausted he barely has time to see the rushing water in his mind's eye before he falls asleep. Others, like Blaine Mayhugh, take medication. Several sleep tepee-style against their wives, as they had when they had huddled together for warmth in the mine. 'It breaks my heart to think what he must have gone through down there,' said one miner's wife. Only the irrepressible Tom Foy claims that he has not had nightmares, citing his experiences in Vietnam as having hardened him for any ordeal.

For all of them, though, it has been a transforming experience, and one for which there are many positive aspects. Perhaps he is superficially unaffected by his experience, but Tom Foy has changed in other ways, now a true believer rather than a man who, for most of his life, paid lip-service to religion. Like most of those involved in this extraordinary story, he now believes in miracles – and in spending time with his family, particularly quad-biking with his grandchildren. Those of the miners who are parents – the majority – are more careful of and sensitive to their children, quicker to hug and slower to scold. They are more demonstrative around their friends, too, appreciating their companionship, as well as the little pleasures and wonders in life like the blue sky and the clouds scudding across the Somerset horizon. Many have made a vow to live the rest of their lives as they used to dine underground – metaphorically eating the dessert first. 'Live for today' has become their motto.

Once the filming, the photo calls, the media events and the obligatory magazine interviews are over, the Quecreek Nine are all looking forward to returning to normal life. For Leslie Mayhugh, it means going back to her Tuesday-night bingo; for John Unger, it means enjoying his farm and savoring time with his friends; while for Robert Pugh it means standing anonymously in the back row during Mass. Now that the hunting season has started they will be able to spend time doing what they love best – hunting and fishing.

Yet, as hard as they may try, life for these men will never truly be the same again. They have become emblems of the kind of America the nation would like to believe in. Randy Fogle's phone still runs red hot with requests for them to attend events as wide-ranging as the Miss America Pageant and a Farm Aid concert. Beyond that, however, they are disciples, living witnesses to a miracle that has drawn thousands to Bill Arnold's farm. Most of these faithful first make their pilgrimage to Shanksville, the crash site of Flight 93, and then to the scene where nine men were plucked from the bowels of the earth. 'When they were digging for the miners it was as if they found the hearts of Flight 93,' said one visitor.

Of these two incidents, one celebrates death and valor, the other life and heroism; both are incredible stories of tragedy and triumph. These two shrines, just ten miles apart, now serve as bookends to the human spirit, to man's humanity and inhumanity. As John Weir says of the Quecreek rescue, 'This miracle is hard to explain. Somerset needed this after Shanksville. America needed heroes. Such a big miracle in such a little town. Makes you think.'

Bill Arnold has already picked the spot at the rescue site on his farm where he will plant nine evergreens linked with a rope to represent the rescued miners who tied themselves together as they awaited their final moments. It is all part of his plan to turn the site into a memorial garden to commemorate the extraordinary events of July 2002. Nine granite boulders will signify the men who escaped, while right at the front and in the center of this garden of remembrance, there will be an oak to symbolize the Lord Our God. Mark Popernack has asked him to get the biggest oak he can find as he firmly believes that it was only divine intervention that saved their lives.

For a few days Bill chewed over what he wanted to have inscribed on a plaque that will have a prominent place in the garden. Inspiration came to him one morning as he was about to feed the cattle. Sitting in his barn, he wrote a single line on the side of a feed bag.

'When there seems to be no life in the oak, His roots run deep.'